Beyond the Wasteland

Beyond the Wasteland

The Criticism of Broadcasting

Revised Edition

Robert Rutherford Smith
Temple University

Speech Communication Association
5105 Backlick Road, Annandale, Virginia 22003

ERIC Clearinghouse on Reading and Communication Skills
National Institute of Education

Speech Communication Association Publications Board: Robert R. Smith, Temple University, *Chairperson;* Hermann Stelzner, University of Massachusetts; Lawrence B. Rosenfeld, University of New Mexico; William Work, Executive Secretary, Speech Communication Association, *ex officio.*

Published 1980 by the ERIC Clearinghouse on Reading and Communication Skills, 1111 Kenyon Road, Urbana, Illinois 61801, and the Speech Communication Association, 5105 E. Backlick Road, Annandale, Virginia 22003. Printed in the United States of America.

 This publication was prepared with funding from the National Institute of Education, U.S. Department of Education, under contract no. 400-78-0026. Contractors undertaking such projects under government sponsorship are encouraged to express freely their judgment in professional and technical matters. Prior to publication, the manuscript was submitted to the Speech Communication Association for critical review and determination of professional competence. This publication has met such standards. Points of view or opinions, however, do not necessarily represent the official view or opinions of either the Speech Communication Association or the National Institute of Education.

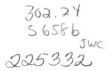

Contents

To my colleagues . . *Sermo Inter Amicos Optima Est*

Revised edition:

To the readers of the first: I'm a bit like Sam at the moment when Hump told him he ought to 'play it' again.

Foreword

A commonplace of the 1980s is to observe that the United States has moved well into a new post-industrial era sometimes called "The Information Society" or "The Age of Communication." Telecommunications, including broadcasting, are playing a major role in that continuing revolution.

We are only beginning to understand the impacts of the electronic mass media on our individual lives and on our social institutions. We know that television and radio are prime sources of information and entertainment in our culture, but we are less certain about their influences on attitudes, beliefs, and values. Without always being able to differentiate cause from effect, we know that "instant" communications significantly affect the very course of history. Media coverage of the Civil Rights movement, the Vietnam War, Watergate, and the Iranian crisis taught us that.

As educators, we are regularly reminded that the young spend more time watching television than they spend in school. We know, therefore, that television is a significant force in the education of children—but we're not always sure *what* is being learned. Our educational concerns also extend to more effective uses of television and radio in direct, classroom instruction. There is growing recognition of the need to harmonize informal, unstructured media learning experiences with those that take place through formal instruction.

For the reasons suggested above, media 'literacy' is an imperative of our time. Television and radio are too pervasive, too influential, to be ignored. Quite apart from the issue of whether broadcasting enriches or pollutes the environment, it will surely continue to be an important social and cultural force.

There are two principal, complementary ways to promote more sophisticated consumption of broadcasting: (1) extensive critical viewing and listening; and (2) exposure to informed critical opinion. This second edition of *Beyond the Wasteland* provides an updated "state of the art" on the criticism of broadcasting. It offers information that will help teachers sharpen their own critical capacities and, in turn, will help them explore the uses of media criticism with their students. *Beyond the Wasteland* also provides important suggestions and contextual insights for the mass media researcher.

This new edition, like its predecessor, is published by the Speech Communication Association in cooperation with the Educational Resources Information Center (ERIC) Clearinghouse on Reading and Communication Skills. It is responsive to a mandate from the National Institute of Education, under whose aegis the ERIC program is administered, to make available to teachers and investigators publications that will help them apply current knowledge more effectively. Through these publications, written by such recognized national authorities as Dean Robert R. Smith, the ERIC system extends its usefulness beyond its basic function of providing a sophisticated educational resources data base.

Broadcasting's movement "beyond the wasteland" has been aided and abetted by informed criticism. Spurred in part by an unending succession of technological advances, we know that the electronic mass media will continue to change—will continue to grow. Media, and the consumers of media, assert reciprocal influences on one another. An enhanced citizen awareness of the principles of broadcasting criticism can help hasten the day when the "wasteland" metaphor will no longer be appropriate. It is toward that end that this book has been written.

William Work, Director
Speech Communication
Module, ERIC/RCS

Preface

Yesterday morning, the CBS-TV morning show featured, among other things, an essay on the political effects of television by Jeff Greenfield. It was a well-researched, carefully argued piece of writing. It was not, however, unusual. Two days earlier I watched Ron Hendron on NBC-TV's *Today Show*. He reviewed a new series on—of all networks—NBC. In a demonstration of editorial integrity that would astonish many print journalists, he trounced the program. Somewhat lighthearted compared with Greenfield's effort, it nevertheless demonstrated a close and careful analysis of the program. On ABC's morning program, Rona Barrett presented a brief photo essay on two leading television performers. Although neither as careful as Greenfield, nor as perceptive as Hendron, it was, in a sense, television criticism. Television criticism has become part of our breakfast routine.

This is a radical change in the four years since the first edition of this book appeared. At that time, I bemoaned the absence of regular, independent published criticism. "Television criticism," I wrote, "is a much neglected form." Perhaps it was.

Yet, in a different sense, television and radio have always had critics. When Commissioner Newton Minow of the Federal Communications Commission (FCC) talked of a "vast wasteland," he was engaging in criticism. When Senator Pastore and the leaders of the citizen's group, Action for Children's Television, criticized the Saturday morning "children's ghetto," they were practicing television criticism. When former Vice President Spiro Agnew attacked television newsreporters such as Dan Rather, he, also, was practicing television criticism. Journalist and consumer affairs specialist Betty Furness, former President Lyndon B. Johnson, Office of Telecommunications Planning head Clay T. Whitehead, Everett Parker of the United Church of Christ—all have functioned as television critics.

One of the oddities of television is that, when we think of criticism, we frequently think of these public figures rather than Harlan Ellison, Les Brown, or others who write criticism in a traditional way. Perhaps published television criticism is weak because there are so many critics in government, in universities, in barbershops, and in millions of homes.

That may be a facile way of explaining the dearth of *published* criticism, however. After all, presidents, professors, barbers, and fathers all criticize sports, and no newspaper of any stature functions without a prosperous and lively sports department in which opinion and colorful writing flourish. No, we can't explain the weakness of television criticism by saying that everyone does it. We must look elsewhere.

One reason may be that the television industry systematically discourages critics. In the mid-1960s, one network purchased a full-page advertisement in the *New York Times* to proclaim that "nobody likes us but people." They proudly pointed out that, although the critics had panned their offerings, their ratings were very high. Such audacity, such brazen contempt for qualitative judgments, is nearly unthinkable in any of the other performing arts.

Not only does the industry discourage criticism, but television itself is very difficult to criticize. It is essentially repetitive. Can a critic, even a tough-skinned, imaginative, dedicated critic, seriously review each program in a comedy series? Would anyone want to read this serial cataloguing of mediocrity? The answer to both questions appears to be no. Critics tend to criticize those programs that are interesting to criticize: specials, major news events, a new series that has been widely promoted, or programs concerning well-known personalities. Most of the programs that most of the people watch most of the time do not lend themselves to thoughtful evaluation.

Lacking programs to interest them, critics frequently turn to the issues that lie behind the programs. Should political candidates be given equal time? Should there be a limit on the number of minutes devoted to advertising in a program? Should the industry employ more members of minority groups? Should citizen groups have more influence on programming? In this way, the critics of broadcasting turn from the programs and enter debates on public policy, politics, the social effects of the media, the ethics of advertising, and other tangential topics. This debate is usually not reported in the daily television column. It appears in academic journals, law journals, elite magazines, the *Congressional Record*, and the publications of action groups. Meanwhile, the programs continue, hour after hour, day after day, without thoughtful criticism.

One interesting development in European and British writing about television is that critics have begun to pay attention to the "flow." Raymond Williams, an English critic, has used the term to mean the rapid passing of units—news items, for instance—making up an overall sense of the program. Others, particularly Finnish scholars, have used the term to point to the flow of American programs onto the screens of other nations, many of them in the Third World. These critics use the concept of flow to demonstrate and argue against American imperialism. Both viewpoints minimize the importance of the individual program by pointing to the vast quantity of programs, arguing that programs are more important in the mass than in the particular.

In these short essays we will be concerned with understanding television criticism as it occurs in America. We will consider the various points of view from which broadcasting can be criticized—from the standpoint of the public policy maker, the social scientist, the audience member, and, of course, the aesthetician. We will also be concerned with the various ways in which critics evaluate the broadcasting industry, government regulators, and programs.

Finally, we will consider the possibility that the absence of criticism may have been beneficial to the development of television. American television is, after all, the most imitated system in the world. Perhaps one of the reasons is that it has grown freely in response to audience and economic pressures. The absence of a humane and civilizing criticism may have fostered an overwhelming concern for programs acceptable to what H. L. Mencken called the "boobocracy,"; it may also have provided an opportunity for popular art to thrive without the restraints of a criticism based on taste, style, and excellence. The absence of television criticism may have allowed television to become our liveliest primitive art.

Reading about criticism, of course, is rather like reading about swimming or dancing. If you don't practice while you read, you won't have much success. To help you along, a few readings have been suggested at the end of each chapter. They are, for the most part, only introductory.

Here, then, are several perspectives on television criticism.

R.S.

I The Process of Criticism

Criticism is a way of behaving. It is the process of relating to the object to be evaluated in a responsive and intelligent manner. The process of criticism is not completed until that response is integrated into prior knowledge of the object, evaluated, and communicated to others. The process of criticism includes perception, integration, evaluation, and expression.

The first part of this book is concerned with the process of criticizing broadcast programs. In it we will consider criticism as a way of knowing, the varieties of criticism, two critical approaches—the mythological and the public policy oriented—and we will end by looking at criteria that have been used by some critics in the past.

The Aims of Criticism

Each of us performs a variety of critical acts each day. Arranging books on our bookshelf is a modest critical activity. Recommending a book, film, or television program to a friend is a more self-conscious variety of criticism. Criticizing a program or defending a program from the attack of someone else is the most obviously critical behavior in which most of us engage. We are all, at some time or other, critics of books, people, films, and television and radio programs. This book is concerned with television and radio criticism.

Although most of us discuss broadcast programs frequently, it is unlikely that we have formulated criteria for evaluating them. We may be self-conscious in discussing literary genre (essays, poetry, fiction, etc.), and we may have a strong sense of the major periods and the prominent writers in each, but it is unlikely that we have a comparable critical apparatus for dealing with radio or television. Broadcasting may be vaguely accused of misleading children, or of being "mediocre," but we seldom make formal critical judgments about programs. They simply exist. We ask little of them, and they demand little of us.

In the following chapters it will be argued that television and radio are complex, that the issues are sometimes central to our notions of democracy and our concern about the First Amendment, and that they offer a window on contemporary culture. The aim of this book is to encourage viewers to listen and view critically. Before we begin, it may be worth spending a few words considering the functions of criticism.

There are at least four ways of knowing—the ways of the scientist, the rhetorician, the mystic, and the critic. Scientists are concerned with explaining data. There are, in science, no experts. A beginner may develop a theory which steals a Nobel prize from world-renowned scientists. James Watson, for instance, was a graduate student when he and his partner developed their explanation of the DNA molecule. In science all opinions are, or ought to be, equal. Eloquence will not create evidence that will fit a faulty theory. Scientists are empirical—they insist upon evidence.

Rhetoricians operate in quite a different way. They acknowledge that opinions are unequal, that ideas have histories that may be important, that arguments may be won by ethos, pathos, or logos. They are concerned with argument, and the winning argument may be based upon ethical appeal rather than a scientist's evidence. Rhetoricians live in a more complex world than scientists, a world in which doubts, irony, and pathos play a part. Nevertheless, rhetoricians can usually relate all evidence, all persuasive devices, and all appeals to the single point being argued. They are concerned with the decision in an argument.

Others may use subjective "evidence." For instance, mystics admit an even greater variety of evidence. Visions, rhetorical devices, and "hard" evidence are all acceptable to mystics. Truth is the criterion used in mystical determinations, and truth is more subjective than evidence, argument, or reason.

Finally, we come to critics. Critics, like mystics and rhetoricians, allow a variety of evidence to be introduced. Aesthetic judgments, social scientific information about media effects, political discussions about public policy, and technological information about the potential of the media are all acceptable to critics of radio or television. Although critics should be fair and accurate in using sources, there is no arbitrary limit upon the kinds of support they can use to inform a critical judgment.

Like scientists, critics consider all opinions, although expert opinion is likely to count for more. If scientists are concerned with explanation, mystics with truth, and rhetoricians with argumentation, critics are concerned with evaluation.

Of course, evaluation by itself is not a very helpful act. If critics behaved like baseball umpires who merely call the pitches without explaining how they arrive at their evaluations, they would be of little use to their readers. Critics must explain their evaluations. If this is done successfully, the result will be a new insight which may aid their readers in making future decisions. This insight is perhaps the greatest contribution critics can make to their readers.

The Aim of the Critic

Critics, while attempting to provide insight and helpful evaluations to readers, may have other aims. They may, for instance, have a strong desire to reform commercial broadcasting. If this is their aim, they will select shows which demonstrate to their readers either the shortcomings of the existing system or, if they find a program which meets their approval, the potentials of the system. Reform of the system is one of the primary aims of a number of critics, such as Robert Lewis Shayon, and groups, such as Action for Children's Television.

Other writers have selected other aims. Horace Newcomb, for instance, has attempted to solve the problem of television criticism by exploring the ways in which television uses history. Others, such as Oscar Handlin and David Manning White, have been interested in the ways in which television and radio have influenced popular culture. Still others have selected as their aim the understanding of the relation of mass communication to traditional culture—Edward Shils comes to mind—while others, such as Ernest Van Den Haag, have been concerned with the social effects of broadcasting and the development of the consensual society. Critics have had commitments to reform, Marxism, high aesthetic standards, the adulation of celebrities, consumers, or the understanding of the medium.

Such aims may exist alongside other, more pragmatic considerations. For example, critics, like other writers, need to find a readership if they are to stay in business. This concern may encourage them to emphasize the journalistically interesting at the expense of the critically important. In addition, critics must be concerned about their reputation among broadcasters.

In short, critics, like other persons, may wear blinders, which may be ideological (Marxism or conservatism), psychological (a preference for certain kinds of concerns), or expedient (a desire to get by-lines and be quoted). These private commitments of critics may give depth to their writing or may limit their vision.

However, a critic is not simply an advocate for a point of view. The role is larger than that of the advocate. Critics must perceive the program being criticized as openly and fairly as possible. Then, they must integrate that perception into their prior knowledge of the subject—its genre, audience, industry economics, and public policy—and they must then evaluate the program by the standards appropriate to it. Theatre critic Stark Young once suggested that the criteria for judging a play are implicit in the play itself. Imagine the play as excellent as it might be, he suggested, and then compare the play as performed with the standard extrapolated from it. Similarly, critics of broadcasting can be urged to judge each program by the standards suggested by the program itself.

Finally, critics must communicate their perception, integration, and evaluation to others. Critics must be variously sensitive and open, analytic, knowledgeable, and, finally, creative in communicating the results of their work. The critical act is not complete until critics have informed, and perhaps persuaded, others.

The Varieties of Criticism

The term "criticism" is applied to a variety of kinds of writing. The consequence is confusion about the purposes of television criticism and the standards which should be applied when evaluating it. After all, an essay on public policy in the *Mother Earth News* should not be considered in the same way as, say, a short blurb summarizing a feature film which might appear in *TV Guide*. In this chapter we will consider the varieties of criticism and the standards appropriate to each.

There are various possible ways in which television criticism could be categorized: by length, by the medium in which it appears, by the author's presumed intention, or by the subject (a program, a personality, a policy) with which it deals. Some criticism is used in making viewing choices; some, as entertainment; some, as a source of news about the industry. We have attempted to group criticism according to the ways in which readers might use it and how it might function for them. The categories are, of course, arbitrary. They will be useful if they lead readers into making distinctions among the varieties of criticism and, perhaps, to creating categories which more nearly describe their own experience as consumers of television criticism.

Previews. The preview is probably the most influential of all forms of criticism. Unlike any of the other kinds, it can influence the viewers' program choices *before* the time of broadcast. Although previews appear before the program is viewed by the audience, we may consider them criticism because they are often based upon a pre-viewing of a tape recording of the show. This is particularly true of previews carried by wire services, such as Associated Press, United Press International, or other syndicated newspaper services. Their writers, usually based in New York or Los Angeles, may have easier access to previewing than writers in other cities.

In local newspapers the preview is frequently based upon a criticism written by a writer for a wire service and rewritten locally. Clearly, local writers are dependent upon second-hand information and their judgments are likely to be questionable.

Another source of information for previews is the press release from a network or local station. Obviously, stations and networks are not impartial sources for critical judgments. Yet, the distortion introduced by source bias is less than might be expected, because networks and stations usually expend their promotional efforts primarily on programs likely to be either popular or critical successes.

Typically, a preview is succinct—fifty words or less is not uncommon—and usually mentions the subject matter and the leading participants and indicates what is of unusual interest in the program. Frequently, these judgments are compressed into a code ("dull," "interesting," or "don't miss") or into symbols (four stars, three stars, etc.).

Previews vary widely in value. In assessing them, it is useful to ask: Is the evaluation based upon a viewing of the program or upon press releases from the producers? Is the preview signed or anonymous? Have other previews from the same source proved valuable to me in my viewing?

Because it is usually short in length, the preview is not a form appropriate for complex arguments or subtle judgments. When it is unsigned, we may not know whether we are getting thinly disguised program advertising or an independent judgment. Despite all these shortcomings, the preview is frequently decisive in viewer decisions about what to watch and deserves analysis.

Gossip Columns. Radio and television personalities are of interest to thousands, and they benefit from any mention they may receive in the press. It is not surprising that many newspapers carry articles in which the personal and professional activities of these personalities are reported. Many stories are unrelated to broadcasting (for instance, where a personality lives or his or her hobbies or political activities). Others, when they report information about how decisions are made about programs, may be useful in understanding broadcasting.

In some newspapers, particularly in smaller cities, human interest items about personalities are intermixed with evaluative comments or reports of the judgments of others, as well as with press releases from stations, and the whole is presented as the work of the "television critic." The unity of such columns is usually derived from the journalistic style of the compiler.

Gossip columns are useful for creating interest in the persons responsible for programs. They may contain information about the industry otherwise unobtainable. To the extent that they substitute criticism of the person for criticism of the program, however, they are useless to the student of broadcasting.

Daily Reviews. A minority of newspapers—the exact number is not known—employ a writer to produce a critical essay on broadcasting two or three times a week. Some of these columns border on the gossip mentioned earlier, while others contain interesting analyses of programs viewed the preceding day.

The best of such critics—Les Brown, Harlan Ellison, and Michael Arlen are among the best practitioners in the recent past—have thoughtfully worked out their critical methods and write as seriously and responsibly as their colleagues who deal with music and theatre.

The daily review typically is concerned with the critical reaction to a single program. The critic may compare a program with others in a series or with other similar programs, but the focus is normally on a single program.

The curse of daily reviewers is that their audience cannot see the program after reading the review. Further, those who have seen the show will already have made their evaluations. If programs were re-run on a regular basis, daily reviewers might have greater influence on viewers or programmers. As it is, they must be content to suggest that their readers seek out or avoid similar programs in the future. It is the fate of these hapless reviewers to be read only after the event by an audience that does not have access to the subject of their writing.

When reading reviews, it may be useful to ask: Does the reviewer have consistent criteria which he or she applies regularly, or does the reviewer write on the basis of unsystematic criteria? Are the suggestions in the review useful in making future viewing decisions? Is there a reviewer whose judgments I find interesting and useful in making my viewing decisions?

Weekly Criticism. The most complex, knowledgeable, and thoughtful criticism frequently appears in weekly or monthly publications such as *TV Guide*, the Sunday *New York Times* entertainment section, *The New Yorker*, and *Variety*. Many magazines, such as *Time* and *Newsweek*, carry regular criticism, while others, such as the *New Republic*, *Cosmopolitan*, *Atlantic Monthly*, or *Harper's Magazine*, carry criticism when there is a program or issue which, in the editors' judgment, is of interest to their readers.

It is in the weekly essay that writers often find that they

can back off from specific programs and consider program trends and issues. It is also here that writers can develop ideas at length.

Although there is no single "best place" to look for such essays, readers who include *TV Guide* and the Sunday *New York Times* entertainment section in their diet will encounter some of the best current essays on television.

In evaluating weekly criticism (or monthly, in the case of some magazines), it may be useful to ask: Has the writer conducted research in the programs or issues he or she is discussing, or does the writer depend upon secondary sources? Are the major issues of the day considered? Are the issues considered of concern to me as a viewer, or do they serve the interests of those in the industry?

What Do Critics Write About?

Although critics of literature and the arts deal with performances, whether written, painted, sung, or played, television critics often devote much of their writing to other matters. Below are some categories which may be useful in analyzing broadcast criticism.

> Program previews.
>
> Program reviews.
>
> Cable distribution systems, their promise and problems.
>
> Industry economics, including advertising, costs, sponsors, etc.
>
> Governmental affairs, including regulatory problems with both the FCC and the Federal Trade Commission (FTC).
>
> Political effects of television and political uses of television.
>
> Personalities, including interviews with stars, broadcasters, executives.
>
> Technical affairs, including new devices and technical problems of covering an unusual event.
>
> Home video recorders and other technological developments.
>
> Program practices and policies, including reasons for program decisions.
>
> Audience matters, including ratings, letters from readers, comments on the audience by broadcasters.
>
> Effects of television, including violence, social change, and so on.

Broadcasting critics include in their writing matters often neglected by critics of other forms. Music critics, for instance, seldom write about the economics of music. This variety gives critics of broadcasting the opportunity to investigate and write about the problems of the day. This is in response, in part, to the sameness of the programs, which discourages serious criticism, and, in part, to audience interests. Many of us find the economics of broadcasting or its alleged effects fascinating, and critics have been quick to cater to that interest.

The Functions of Criticism

As we have suggested above, many critics write as guides for viewers. Others try to convey information which may be of interest to viewers. Still others have assigned themselves more ambitious tasks: to address the industry and encourage reform, to alert consumers to what they may expect and may or may not receive from broadcasting, or to make sense of radio and television as forms of popular art.

In an article in the *Journal of Broadcasting*, Peter Mayeux analyzed the stated and manifest functions of three television critics: Jack Gould, Larry Wolter, and Hal Humphrey.[1] He reported that the three critics indicated that the functions of critics should be "to inform the reader about the events of broadcasting, to act as 'mediator' between the viewing public and the television industry, and to serve as a catalyst for better programming and the full use of the potential of the television medium." In evaluating their criticism, Mayeux noted that they tended to "talk directly to the industry to improve television, and to inform and entertain the reading public." It is interesting to note that two of their manifest functions—talking directly to the industry and entertaining—were not among their stated functions.

Other critics have chosen to describe their functions in different ways. Some have attempted to work out a television aesthetic, some have attempted to bring broadcasting into the intellectual life of the twentieth century, and others have attempted to alert their readers to television's role in the events of our time.

Harlan Ellison, television critic for the Los Angeles *Free Press*, prefaced a collection of his criticism with this warning:

> But make no mistake. I am not *really* talking about TV here.
> I am talking about dissidence, repression, censorship, the bru-

> tality and stupidity of much of our culture, the threat of the
> Common Man, the dangers of being passive in a time when
> the individual is merely cannon-fodder, the lying and cheating
> and killing our "patriots" do in the sweet name of the Amer-
> ican Way.[2]

Ellison emphasizes issues in his writing, providing very little information about the industry and constantly prodding his readers
to consider what television is doing for them and to them.

There has been, since Gilbert Seldes first suggested that Krazy
Kat was, or at least had the potential to be, as significant as any
specific example of High Art, an interest in developing aesthetic
criteria for film and broadcasting. In 1962 Robert Lewis Shayon,
former television critic for the *Saturday Review*, edited a collection of essays concerned with television as art. In it a diverse
group of writers, including Moses Hadas, Marya Mannes, Tyrone
Guthrie, Ashley Montague, Walter Cronkite, and George Balanchine,
considered the status of television at that time. Re-reading the
collection is an astonishing experience, primarily because most of
the problems the writers identify remain unsolved and most of the
potential they identify in television remains unrealized.   After
noting that "something must happen to give television a chance
to develop in its own style, using the arts of the past, as a child,
in order to become a separate individual," Gilbert Seldes went
on to note:

> Television may flourish without such an individual
> development—and still make a lot of money. But it will
> not have the final interest that silent movies had and
> radio promised to develop. It will be a complex of
> techniques which have not fused into an art.[3]

As one reads the essays in the book, one is left with the feeling
that television did not develop as Seldes and others hoped it would.

This does not mean that television, or those in the audience,
have failed. Horace Newcomb, in an essay entitled "Toward a Television Aesthetic," noted that the central weakness of television
is the "lack of artistic probability."[4]:

> Because the shows conclude dramatically at the end of a single
> episode, and because the necessity for a popular response calls
> for an affirmative ending, we lose sight of the true complexity
> of many of the issues examined.[5]

He notes that this could be overcome by having different kinds
of problems in each episode, and by allowing the characters and
the situation to grow and change. For example, Richie's decision

to go to college, in *Happy Days*, could allow him to develop and could enlarge the content of the series. Newcomb recognizes television's aesthetic use of history, in which

> we see families in domestic comedy behave as if they live in an idealized nineteenth-century version of America. . . . As if our time somehow mythically coexisted with that of an easier age, we create forms that speak in opposition to their contemporary settings.[6]

Television, in Newcomb's view, remakes both our own contemporary life and history. It relates them in ways which he thinks misleading in public affairs, although possibly helpful in pointing to the continuities in human life. *MASH*, for instance, or *Hogan's Heroes*, may falsify war but point to enduring human concerns and qualities such as status competition, sex and friendship.

Critics who insist on accuracy in both historical and contemporary programs are, of course, at odds with Newcomb. Michael J. Arlen, for instance, argues that

> Television has a transforming effect on events. It has a transforming effect on the people who watch the transformed events— it's just hard to know what that is, and hard, too, to believe that either the demonologists or those happy McLuhanesque embraces of modernism get one much closer toward finding out, although I could be wrong about that.[7]

In summary, television criticism may function to pass information to the audience, to spur the industry, to work out a new aesthetic, or to help audience members become aware of what's happening because of broadcasting.

The Future of Broadcasting Criticism

In an essay in the *Journal of Broadcasting*, Maurice Shelby reported that a study of patterns in broadcasting criticism over a thirty-year period revealed a sixfold increase in the quantity of criticism.[8] He also noted that criticism has become more critical and less neutral with the passage of time and that critics have tended to write about topics of national rather than local interest.

What does this suggest for the future of broadcasting criticism? One might postulate increasing negativism and a larger amount of criticism as weekly special-interest newspapers multiply. It is difficult to look to the future of criticism, however, because we have no tradition on which to base our projections. The absence of a tradition is perhaps the most important characteristic of television and radio criticism. In its absence, one can assume little about the future except that critical discussion will be sorely needed. As Moses Hadas has written, "The larger and more indiscriminate the audience, the greater the need to safeguard and purify standards of quality and taste."[9]

There is some evidence that critics, by emphasizing the reviews of new program series, may miss opportunities for analysis of the issues. Jules Rossman, in a study of television critics in the top ten markets, found that "public television programs constituted about 10% of each critic's total reviews, new series about 41%, and specials only 21%." In his conclusion he noted that, "while critics doubt their influence on programmers, government decision makers, or viewers, their columns still do not emphasize the kind of content which *could* influence."[10]

The student of the criticism of broadcasting may find the absence of a canon confusing, the absence of standards for both television and its critics dismaying, and the expanse of territory available for criticism numbing. Although the absence of classics, established categories, and well-defined criteria makes the field difficult to approach, the opportunities make it inviting. As Gilbert Seldes noted, "television's true literature has, in fact, yet to be written."

Notes

1. Peter E. Mayeux, "Three Television Critics: Stated vs. Manifest Functions," *Journal of Broadcasting* 14 (Winter 1969-1970): 25-36.

2. Harlan Ellison, *The Glass Teat* (New York: Ace Publishing Company, 1969), pp. 11-12.

3. Gilbert Seldes, "Beg, Borrow—or Annex," in *The Eighth Art*, ed. Robert Lewis Shayon (New York: Holt, Rinehart and Winston, 1962), pp. 107-108.

4. Horace Newcomb, *TV the Most Popular Art* (New York: Anchor Books, 1974), pp. 254-256.

5. Ibid., p. 260.

6. Ibid.

7. Michael J. Arlen, *Living-Room War* (New York: Tower Publications, 1968), p. 11.

8. Maurice E. Shelby, Jr., "Patterns in Thirty Years of Broadcast Criticism," *Journal of Broadcasting* 11 (Winter 1966-1967): 27-40.

9. Moses Hadas, "Climate of Criticism," in *The Eighth Art*, ed. Robert Lewis Shayon (New York: Holt, Rinehart and Winston, 1962), p. 16.

10. Jules Rossman, "The TV Critic Column: Is It Influential?" *Journal of Broadcasting* 19 (Fall 1975): 401-411.

Suggested Readings

Arlen, Michael J. *Living-Room War*. New York: Tower Publications, 1968. His collective criticism, including television and Vietnam.

Arlen, Michael J. *The View From Highway 1: Essays on Television*. New York: Farrar, Staus & Giroux, 1976. More, including brilliant variations on conventional forms of criticism.

Brown, Les. *Television*. New York: Harcourt Brace Jovanovich, 1971. The former *Variety* television reporter, now critic for the *New York Times*, introduced the business. More criticism than text, he provides insights into how things are and why they got that way.

Casty, Alan. *Mass Media and Mass Man*. New York: Holt, Rinehart and Winston, 1968. A collection of essays, now somewhat dated, that raises the social questions with which critics were concerned in the years immediately preceding publication. Includes Ernest Van Den Haag's memorable "Of Happiness and Despair We Have No Measure."

Cater, Douglas and Richard Adler. *Television as a Social Force: New Approaches to TV Criticism*. New York: Praeger Publishers, 1975. A selection of perceptive essays by Paul Weaver, Kas Kalba, Michael Novak and others.

Cater, Douglas and Richard Adler. *Television as a Cultural Force*. New York: Praeger Publishers, 1976. A sequel to the above, including essays, including David Littlejohn, Peter Wood and a useful reading list by Christopher Sterling. Both of these books were sponsored by the Aspen Institute for Humanistic Studies.

Ellison, Harlan. *The Glass Teat*. New York: Ace Publishing Company, 1969. Sixty-ish book, in manner and content. Ellison is an excellent analyst of the media.

Hazard, Patrick D. *TV as Art: Some Essays in Criticism*. Urbana, Illinois: National Council of Teachers of English, 1966. Essays that relate conceptually to literary studies. Now dated, but some of the concerns endure.

Jacobs, Norman. *Culture for the Millions*. Boston: Beacon Press, 1964. Report of a conference sponsored by the Tamiment Institute and the Journal of the American Academy of Arts and Sciences in June 1959. A very useful collection including essays by Leo Rosten, Oscar Handlin, and Hannah Arendt, and Randall Jarrell's "A Sad Heart at the Supermarket."

Mander, Jerry. *Four Arguments for the Elimination of Television*. New York: William Morrow and Co., 1978. A series of wild and crazy essays that go far beyond the evidence in ascribing the ills of our society to television. Good for discussion.

Newcomb, Horace. *TV the most Popular Art*. New York: Anchor, 1974. One of the most intelligent and thoughtful books concerning television to appear in recent years.

Primeau, Ronald. *The Rhetoric of Television*. New York: Longmans, 1979.
    An attempt to apply concepts from other fields, with many useful exam-
    ples. A useful glossary and bibliography is included.

Schwartz, Tony. *The Responsive Chord*. New York: Anchor Books, 1973.
    Schwartz, an experienced producer, has an intuitive grasp of the potential
    of the broadcast media that makes for exciting reading. One of the few
    post-McLuhan books of criticism.

Seldes, Gilbert. *The Great Audience*. New York: The Viking Press, 1951.
    One of the two or three most significant books in the development of
    criticism of broadcasting. Seldes was the *Saturday Review* critic, among
    other appointments.

Shayon, Robert Lewis, ed. *The Eighth Art*. New York: Holt, Rinehart and
    Winston, 1962. A book that wears well, containing essays by Hadas,
    Balanchine, and others.

Shayon, Robert Lewis. *Open to Criticism*. Boston: Beacon Press, 1971. An
    exploration of the problems and potentialities of television that was much
    underrated at the time of publication.

Skornia, Harry J. *Television and Society*. New York: McGraw-Hill, 1965.
    An angry review of the American broadcasting industry and its relation
    to society. Should be read in conjunction with more recent studies on
    effects.

Williams, Raymond. *Television: Technology and Cultural Form*. New York:
    Schocken Books, 1975. The English critic takes on the popular notion
    that television causes social change and assorted other ideas about tele-
    vision and places them in a humanistic perspective. Readers will have to
    make their own application to the American scene.

Mythology and the Criticism of Broadcasting

On a typical weekday evening, more than sixty million people will watch American television for at least part of the evening hours. The programs they watch will often be repetitive situation comedies, detective stories, adventure series, or news programs in which the same reporters return daily to tell them about the activities of a surprisingly stable cast of public figures. The programs change very little from day to day or week to week.

One possible response to this sameness, reminiscent of a Detroit assembly line, is boredom. Another is engaging in an analysis of the economics, regulation, or sociology of the broadcasting industry. Some critics, however, have been intrigued by the sameness, suspecting that the heroes, villains, and repetitive plots must have a meaning for audiences not revealed by casual analysis. They have argued that things are not as they seem.

If not, precisely how *are* they? Television programs are similar, beneath their seeming variety, in the kinds of people, objects and settings which they present. For instance, Walter Cronkite is like a distant uncle who gives us reliable judgments on family matters—like a sage who understands the world, like a wise man who can show us the way. Deodorants and toothpastes are like panaceas, like secret formulas, like small miracles that allow the actors with clean bodies and sparkling teeth to overcome the physical problems common to all of us. Newscasters, advertising products, and television heroes and villains are meaningful to us because they evoke memories of similar persons and problems we have encountered in our work, our families, and our dreams.

Critics interested in the ways in which the persons and plots on television are related to older, mythic structures have borrowed heavily from anthropologists and literary scholars. In many instances the same language is used. In this chapter we will examine the methods of myth criticism and relate them to radio and television programs.

Symbols: Personal, Social, and Archetypical

A symbol is a word, thing, or person that "stands for" something or someone else. Myth critics have been concerned with three kinds of symbols: the personal, the social, and the archetypical.

Personal symbols are those which have intense meaning for one person or a small group, but not for most other people. A lock of hair from a loved one is a conventional—not to say trite— personal symbol. Other personal symbols are a horseshoe from a favorite horse, a gift of small value but great meaning from a friend, a key for a room or house in which something of private significance happened, a word—perhaps a nickname—which evokes reminders of a private meaning, or a person who reminds us of someone who helped or threatened us at some time in the past. Personal symbols are usually unique to the individual or small group which responds to them. Since they are not widely understood, they are of little use in mass communication.

Personal symbols may be found among souvenirs kept for private reasons. The souvenir industry is a large one, however, and deals with symbols widely used in a conventional way. Called social symbols, they include postcards of Niagara Falls, which conveniently suggest a honeymoon; pottery from Mexico, which symbolizes a simpler culture for American tourists; and the Hawaiian lei, which symbolizes acceptance for tourists.

Social symbols are not limited to souvenirs, however. The sceptre represents the authority and power of a king. Two fingers raised in a "V" stood for victory in World War II when used by Winston Churchill and solidarity when used by members of the anti-war movement in the 1960s. A captain's bars or a priest's collar represent membership and rank in a specialized organization and evokes quite different but widely shared responses. A Cadillac or Mercedes Benz represents affluence, but a motorcyle ridden by a black-leathered cyclist stands for something quite different. Most of us respond similarly to these symbols. Most important, even when we have a private reaction— such as a Volkswagon owner who regards Cadillacs as "road hogs"—we are aware of the social meaning of the symbol.

There are some symbols which have remarkable endurance. We read with personal understanding Matthew Arnold's references to the sea in "Dover Beach." We climb mountains to prove our strength and skill and assign the Abominable Snowman to the higher reaches of the earth, alongside Zeus. Clouds have represented freedom from the affairs of humans for generations of people. Old men have been associated with wisdom, snakes with the dark side of events, and birds with peace for a very long time. These symbols, which appear in many cultures over extended periods of time, are termed archetypical symbols. They are simple and basic. Often, they provide the basis for social symbols. For example, people have been swept down river by logs, by barges, by canoes, and by kayaks—underlying all of these social symbols is the archetypical symbol of the river.

Radio and television, which attempt to be instantly intelligible to millions, deal primarily with social symbols. If we glance at the advertising in a back issue of a magazine or at an old movie on television, we can see how quickly social symbols change. Dances which initially cause parents to become concerned about their children quickly become acceptable. Flappers, in old photographs, no longer appear sexy. Giant dams, which once symbolized our technological prowess, have come to be regarded as symbols of waste and indifference to our environment. Social symbols change as the society which uses them changes.

One reason for rapid change in social symbols in our society is mass communication. Radio and television, which help make us aware of new social symbols, also help us become tired of older social symbols. Underlying most social symbols, no matter how new, will be found the archetypical symbols which endure.

One of the easiest ways to identify the use of social and archetypical symbols in broadcasting is to study commercials. The short time available for the message forces the producers of commercials to use the most obvious and current social symbols: boats, bicycles, and swimming pools as symbols for affluent fun; stereotypes in dress as a shorthand for social class; ritualized male and female activities—whether liberated or traditional— to suggest the ways in which the product is used. In commercials, people are peaceful beside the sea, free on skis, sexy in "natural" settings, relaxed about campfires in the summer and fireplaces in the winter, paternal in showing children how to fish. Commercials are shorthand devices for relating the potent emotions associated with parenthood, love, sex, greed, status, and social acceptance to the sponsor's products. They are the Greek vases or Navajo sand paintings of our time—they give meaning to the ephemeral by relating it to the timeless.

Ritual and Mystique

Symbols are static. Although they may be used in a narrative, a device used in most programs, they do not contain an implicit story. In radio and television stories and commercials, something usually happens—a detective finds the criminal, an interviewer challenges a guest, a contestant wins or fails to win a prize.

The "something that happens" in a broadcast program is usually not novel or unexpected. Would you enjoy a quiz program if most of the contestants lost most of the time? Or an adventure series in which the heroes were defeated most of the time? This need for predictability results in a sameness of plot and format that satisfies the casual viewer and may prove frustrating to the critic. We may be able to further our understanding if we ignore the minor differences between programs and concentrate on those things which occur in each episode. This repetitive content is often ritualistic in nature.

A ritual may be thought of as an act, or series of acts, which brings about a satisfactory resolution of the problem with which the program deals. Each day, for instance, a broadcaster on a news program gives narrative shape to the day's events and introduces reports from outside the studio. And detectives often bring their criminals to the police, or into the courtroom, giving ritual closure to the pursuit of justice.

Rituals are varied from program to program but are consistent within programs. Mike Wallace ritualistically challenges his interview guests, pressing them to reveal aspects of personalities otherwise hidden. Dick Cavett, differently but equally ritualistically, establishes a sympathetic rapport that encourages guests to relax and share confidences with the interviewer and the audience. Tom Snyder spars with his guests, changing his role with each new guest.

Commercials are similarly concerned with rituals—for example, getting the washing machine repaired brings sound advice on soaps, and the rush of breakfast repeatedly emphasizes the need for convenient foods. The list can be easily extended.

Most programs are concerned with an underlying similarity from one program to the next which can be called ritual. Although the news may vary from day to day, and the problem in a situation comedy from week to week, the basic ritual must remain unchanged. The newscaster must bid viewers goodnight, the family must come together, and the criminal must be caught if the expectations of viewers are to be met.

In most programs there is a group of persons, a device, or an event which re-occurs in each program and which serves to bring about the resolution of the problem. Batman and Robin emerge when two otherwise unremarkable young men go to the Bat Cave. Clark Kent develops astonishing power when he changes clothes in a telephone booth. This is also true of commercials—cavities are prevented when a particular toothpaste is used as part of a regular program of dental care, a deodorant can cause an unlikely increase in poise and self-confidence. In each of these cases, the device or event brings about changes not to be explained by simple logic. The belief in this potential change is often called the "mystique."

A few of the most obvious instances of mystique were mentioned above. Others may be less obvious. Preparing for surgery may cause physicians to put aside their personal concerns and achieve remarkable healing. When Owen Marshall has a confidential discussion with a client, reality is clarified.

In public affairs programs, such as "Meet the Press," there is within the ritual questioning of public officials an occasional moment in which a reporter scores with a particularly revealing question. The mystique associated with the disinterested news reporter in pursuit of truth gives form and dramatic interest to otherwise shapeless interviews. Rituals and events which possess a mystique are not unique to broadcasting. They relate to age-old stories. Among those which have their roots in the past are the following: tests of bravery (sports and public affairs programs, adventure documentaries, and fictional programs concerned with adventure); the exercise of parental guidance and love (family programs, daytime serials); the demonstration of wisdom or professional competence (medical and legal programs); punishment of the guilty (detective and police shows); atonement for sins (daytime serials); surrender to fortune (game shows); redemption of those who have lost faith (medical and legal programs); the demonstration of wisdom (news programs); and purification (television health product and grooming commercials).

Myths

We began discussing symbols and moved to rituals and their associated mystiques. Although these elements are present in programs, they are not sufficient to explain the attraction programs have for audiences. We watch programs, at least in part, to enjoy the narratives they contain. Often the source of these narratives can be found in the commonly shared myths of our culture.

What is a myth? This definition is by Rollo May:

> Now the myth is a story in which the symbols are brought to-
> gether and are portrayed in the experiences of a living person.
> A myth embodies the symbol [and the ritual] in historical ex-
> perience and forms it into a drama which carries the values
> of our society. We find our myths all about us in the unconscious
> assumptions of our culture; we mould the myths and we use them
> as images in which we can recognize ourselves, our friends, and
> our fellows; we use them as guidelines to our ways of life.[1]

The term myth is sometimes used as a synonym for "false" or "fictional," but such usages miss the point of myth-making. A myth is not testable by evidence.[2] It is simply a phantasmagoric story—Carl Jung called it a dream sequence—shared by a group of people. Myths are large, primitive stories which can be end-lessly retold with slight variations of plot or character. Although the social symbols used in telling a myth may change, the under-lying story endures.

Critics interested in identifying the mythic content of broad-casting will quickly find that in commenting on their findings they are drawn into making a theoretical commitment. They may, with Carl Jung, assign psychoanalytic meanings to their findings, or they may follow Ernst Cassirer and relate myths to political life. They may follow the lead of Claude Levi-Strauss and attempt to find the common structures of popular programs, or they may relate contemporary myths to the historical myths—primarily Greek—which have influenced our literature and drama. For our purposes, an awareness of the mythic content of broad-casting provides a basis for criticism.

Northrop Frye has identified four phases of the "one story" in which he has argued all stories are embedded:

> The dawn, spring, and birth phase, in which generation, revival,
> and resurrection are celebrated.
> The summer, marriage, and triumph phase, in which the hero
> enters paradise. Comedy is often based upon this portion of
> the story.
> The autumn and death phase, which concerns dying gods, vio-
> lence, and sacrifice. Tragedy is based upon this phase of the
> one story.
> The winter and dissolution phase, in which floods, chaos, and
> defeat occur.[3]

Many radio and television programs can be related to this kind of analysis. For example, family programs, such as "The Waltons," "Ozzie and Harriet," and "Sanford and Son," are illustrations of the summer phase; detective programs often illustrate the autumn phase of the story; and advertising, even when it is directed at the elderly or others who may be in the autumn or winter phase of their personal stories, usually involves a summer phase story of triumph made possible by using the product being advertised.

Those who wish to relate contemporary myths to older myths will find that the correspondences offer insights into popular programs. Following are a few comparisons that may lead to critical viewing:

The Myth of Armageddon (the name given in the Apocalypse to the place where the last great battle between nations before Judgment Day was fought): concerns about floods, tornadoes, and other disasters on newscasts; programs concerning overpopulation, food shortages, the arms race; stories concerning pollution, inadvertent poisoning caused by technological progress (atomic waste disposal or possible damage to the ozone caused by jets at high altitudes or aerosol cans).

The Myth of Paradise (distinct from Utopia; originally the pleasure places of the Persian kings; applied to heaven by Christian writers; Dante's *Divine Comedy* concerns a journey through ten spheres of paradise): advertising concerning family events, particularly at holidays such as Christmas; stories placed in suburbs in which community support for the family is present or in urban apartments in which friends provide help; advertising and stories concerning the advantages of wilderness and outdoor activities.

The Myth of Sisyphus (avaricious legendary King of Corinth; father of Ulysses; made to roll a stone to the top of a hill and to retrieve it when it rolls down; his labor is incessant): stories in which the hero carries on his or her role with little reward; daytime serial heroines who hold families together despite domestic entropy; news stories of migrant farm workers and others who endure without adequate compensation. "Hulk" is an example.

The Myth of Prometheus (stole fire from heaven and gave it to men, for which he was punished by Zeus by being chained to Mt. Caucasus where an eagle devoured his liver each night after it was replenished each day; often used as a synonym for inspiration): stories concerning alienated heroes; urban and western gangs; outlaws.

The Myth of Dionysus (Greek name for Bacchus, the god of fertility, wine, and drama): variety shows featuring rock groups; news stories emphasizing group disorders; advertising in which a product is used in the context of a festival or party or euphoric event such as downhill skiing or motorcycling.

The Myth of Sibling Rivalry (the use of a sibling as a benchmark for achievement, as a rival, or as a source of anguish, as Cain and Abel): sports contests; political contests on news or dramatic programs; banter between newscasters; neighbors trying a new product.

The preceding list exhausts neither the classical myths nor the possible instances of their appearances in radio and television programs. It does suggest that, underlying the superficial variety of heroes, there is a unifying mythic structure that extends back through history.

Not all myths, of course, have classical antecedents. Some myths of more recent invention include:

The Myth of Progress: new products with a "better idea"; new governmental programs; political reform; scientific progress.

The Myth of the State: stories of patriotism and struggles for national identity.

The Myth of Youth: innocents as a source of integrity for jaded adults; the influence of children; stories about the group solidarity of young people.

This, also, is an incomplete list, but it may prove helpful in pointing toward the kinds of mythic content which are available for analysis.

The Usefulness of Myth Criticism

The study and practice of myth criticism is useful for learning something of the continuity of our culture and its relation to ages past. The primary benefit, however, is a better understanding of what one scholar has termed "our symbolic environment." Broadcasting supplies us with the symbols of affluence and poverty, masculinity and femininity, and family and society which we use in our everyday life. If we remain unaware of the symbols and myths provided so abundantly by the media, we are, to some extent, using social coins of unknown value.

Programs are unyielding to analysis only if we insist on dealing with them atomically, one by one. If we look for the underlying rhythms that tie them to one another and to the stories of past cultures, both literate and illiterate, we may find that they lead us into the rich tapestry of the Western tradition. If we can see through the idiosyncracies of each program to its underlying structure, we may find that it takes on new meaning, or rather, the meaning it has for us becomes clear.

The seeming atomic existence of individual programs may serve as a metaphor for our own lives. We live more in the "now" and have a greater sense of being different from our ancestors than any previous generation. A consciousness of the ways in which the newest of heroes on the newest of media connect with past generations may help us to develop an awareness of the longer and larger rhythms of our own existences. Criticism concerned with myth helps us to understand not only television but our own lives as well.

Notes

1. Rollo May, *Existential Psychotherapy* (Toronto: CBC Learning Systems, 1967), p. 22.
2. See Kenneth L. Woodward, Susan Malsch, and Diane Camper, "Bite the Bullet, Lone Ranger," *Newsweek* 86 (April 7, 1975): 90-91, for an illustration of an attempt to apply historical evidence as a test of myth.
3. Northrop Frye, *The Archetypes of Literature, Myth and Symbol* (Lincoln: University of Nebraska Press, 1966).

Suggested Readings

Barthes, Roland. *Mythologies.* Translated by Annette Lavers. New York: Mill and Wang, 1973. The leading French *mythologiste* provides a theoretical statement and illustrations from his popular writing. Of major importance, but suffers from poor translation and illustrations drawn exclusively from the French experience.

Bettelheim, Bruno. *The Uses of Enchantment: the Meaning of Fairy Tales.* New York: Random House, 1977. Beguiling essays which encourage the devotion of attention to the latent content of narratives.

Bush, Douglas. *Mythology and the Romantic Tradition in English Poetry.* Cambridge: Harvard University Press, 1937. Overwhelming but useful for alerting critics to parallels with contemporary culture.

Campbell, Joseph. *The Hero with a Thousand Faces.* New York: Pantheon Books, 1949.

Campbell, Joseph. *The Masks of God: Primitive Mythology.* New York: Viking Press, 1959. First of a four-part study of myth. This volume is perhaps the most useful, containing a discussion of "The Psychology of Myth" and "The Functioning of Myth."

Campbell, Joseph. *The Masks of God: Creative Mythology.* New York: Viking Press, 1968. Leads the reader to summary questions and future possibilities.

Campbell, Joseph, ed. *Myths, Dreams and Religions.* New York: E. P. Dutton and Company, 1970. Attempts by contemporary writers, including Alan

Watts, Norman Brown, and Rollo May, to summarize the usefulness of myth analysis in their fields.

Cassirer, Ernst. *Language and Myth*. New York: Dover Publications, 1946. Deals with the "mythic state of mind" and the functions of language. One need not agree to learn from the clear analysis.

Cassirer, Ernst. *The Myth of the State*. Garden City, New York: Doubleday and Company, 1955. A major study of the political implications of myth analysis.

Edmondson, Madeleine, and David Rounds. *The Soaps: Daytime Serials of Radio and TV*. New York: Stein and Day, 1973. A good introduction to the form which provides a rich subject for myth analysis.

Fishwick, Marshall. *The Hero, American Style*. New York: David McKay Company, 1969. A rambling survey of American heroic types: cavaliers, swashbucklers, jolly giants, etc. Though not clearly argued, it contains many suggestions for further study.

Frazer, Sir James George. *The Golden Bough*. New York: The Macmillan Company, 1958. The nineteenth-century pioneer's major study is still highly regarded (although frequently amended by anthropologists) and readable.

Freud, Sigmund. *On Dreams*, ed. James Strachey. New York: The Norton Library, 1952. A popular summary of his *The Interpretation of Dreams* which provides some analytical tools applicable to television.

Frye, Northrop. *Anatomy of Criticism*. Princeton, New Jersey: Princeton University Press, 1957. An influential non-psychiatric theoretical statement on the narrative function and structure of myth.

Harmon, James. *The Great Radio Heroes*. Garden City, New York: Doubleday and Company, 1967. A sentimental review of radio heroes; supplies the overview helpful in analyzing specific older programs. The author is reverential rather than analytic.

Hughes, Richard E. *The Lively Image: Four Myths in Literature*. Cambridge, Massachusetts: Winthrop Publishers, 1975. His introduction, "Approaching Myth," is very useful. Although concerned with the appearances of the four myths (Narcissus, Dionysus, Orpheus, and Christ) in literature, he writes with an awareness of other aspects of American culture.

Jung, Carl, ed. *Man and His Symbols*. New York: Dell Publishing, 1968. Readable popularization of his analytic psychology, with numerous illustrations. Feminists will find much to disagree with, and all will find it provides a structure for criticism of mass media.

Levi-Strauss, Claude. *The Savage Mind*. Chicago: University of Chicago Press, 1966. The innovator in structural analysis of myth uses anthropological data to support his thesis.

Maranda, Pierre, ed. *Mythology*. Baltimore, Maryland: Penguin Books, 1972. A well-chosen collection of essays by Cassirer, Levi-Strauss, and others, providing a broad survey. Neglects mass media.

Murray, Henry A., ed. *Myth and Mythmaking*. New York: George Braziller, Inc., 1960. An older reader, somewhat dated, but containing useful essays by Harry Levin, Northrop Frye, Philip Rieff, and Marshall McLuhan.

Olson, Paul A., ed. *The Uses of Myth*. Report of the Dartmouth Seminar Study Group on Myth. Urbana, Illinois: National Council of Teachers of English, 1968. The position paper by Albert L. Lavin is a useful summary of myth study at that time.

Passman, Arnold. *The Deejays*. New York: The Macmillan Company, 1971. A literate survey of deejays with an awareness of their roles as "tribal chieftains" of the young.

Sebeok, Thomas, ed. *Myth: A Symposium*. Bloomington: Indiana University Press, 1972. A collection of overviews, less technical than Maranda, less readable than Murray. Does not deal with mass media.

The Structuralist Critics and Broadcasting

As we noted earlier, the individual programs in a television series are different in only the most superficial sense. The plots may differ from show to show, week to week, but the narratives—the stories—have a striking similarity. For instance, last week Dan Tanna, the detective hero of *Vega$*, helped a rich woman whose husband thought she had betrayed him. This week, his secretary is about to marry when Tanna realizes that the groom is responsible for the murder of a young woman two years earlier. The stories appear to be different, but in each program Tanna assists a woman who is either misunderstood or misunderstands her true situation. In each program there is a puzzle, a solution based on Tanna's unique knowledge of the city and unerring judgment of people, and a confrontation in which Tanna risks his life to subdue the male adversary. Although each program is different, they are, in their underlying pattern, all the same.

These similarities have been neglected in broadcast criticism. Some critics, notably those interested in the myth content, have begun to look into these similarities. To detect these underlying "structures," one needs to learn to "read" television as one would a poem or a complex musical composition.

Fortunately for us, television critics are not carrying the full burden of pioneering in this field. In a number of fields, notably literature and anthropology, substantial progress has been made in clarifying these methods. We are the lucky inheritors of this work, and our task is simply to apply it to television.

What Is Structuralism?

"Structuralism," English critic Terence Hawkes has written, "is fundamentally a way of thinking about the world which is predominantly concerned with the perception and description of structures. . . ."[1] He continues:

28

> As a developing concern of modern thinkers since Vico, it is the
> result of a momentous historic shift in the nature of perception
> which finally crystallized in the early twentieth century, par-
> ticularly in the field of the physical sciences, but with a mo-
> mentum that has carried through to most other fields.

Ending his attempt at a brief definition, Hawkes notes "the true
nature of things may be said to lie not in things themselves, but in
the relationships which we construct, and then perceive, *between*
them."

Structuralism, then, is a way of perceiving, of thinking. It is not
limited to criticism of television, but may take as its object history,
literature, any of the sciences or the social sciences. Some subjects,
such as chemistry, teach their structures as essential introductory
knowledge. In other fields, such as history, the structuralist revolution is just beginning to be felt.

Some writers, such as Philip Pettit, take a more limited view of
the domain of the structuralists.

> I do not take it to embrace every science, even every human
> science, which claims to investigate 'structures'. . . . Structuralism
> borrows the linguistic model of language and tries to fit this, in
> one way or another, to non-linguistic areas; the idea is that the
> model should suggest lines of empirical analysis. I want to exam-
> ine the different ways in which the linguistic model can be fitted
> to other areas. . . .[2]

Structuralism is a way of thinking about objects which emphasizes their underlying articulations or structures. It begins with
language, partly because of the backgrounds of its pioneers,
partly because the structure of language provides a paradigm for
understanding the structures of other phenomena.

The Linguistic Model

Although it is possible to find elements of structuralist analysis in
Aristotle and St. Augustine's *Confessions*, the first modern writers
to develop this point of view self-consciously were the Swiss lin-
guist Ferdinand de Saussure and the American Charles Sanders
Peirce. It was Peirce who coined the term semiotics, the study of
sign systems. The development of the field of semiotics, closely
related to structuralism, is primarily a development of Peirce's
basic concepts.

The linguistic model to which Pettit referred above is complex. A few key terms will, however, provide access to the literature noted in the bibliography.

Signifier, signified and the sign. Saussure argued that a *signifier* has a physical existence, for instance, a designer label on a pair of jeans worn by a slender young woman. The *signified* is a concept such as fashion, contemporaneity, and high price. The *sign* is the "associative total" of the two: a contemporary life style that includes expensive clothes, a concern for fashion, and, perhaps, taste in music and attitudes toward sex and drugs. Such sign systems are common in advertising. One cigarette company, noting "you've come a long way, baby," uses a cigarette in the hands of an attractive, well-groomed young woman as a *signifier.* The concept *signified* is liberation, freedom from older restraints such as the traditional restriction on smoking in public for women. The *sign*, the associative total, is that smoking demonstrates and embodies the qualities of the new roles women have begun to play. The virtue of this kind of analysis is that it makes the relations of the components of the sign easily apparent and leads one to question whether it is in the interest of women to use smoking as a *sign.*

Indexical and iconic signs. Indexical signs are those in which the sign necessarily varies in direct relation to changes in the object for which it is an index. Mercury in a bulb thermometer, for instance, varies with the temperature and is a good indexical sign of the presence or absence of heat. Perspiration is an index of heat or stress. The applause of a concert audience is an index of its approval.

Iconic signs function differently from indexical signs. Iconic signs represent the visual appearance of the signified. Family snapshots, for instance, are valued insofar as they are iconic. If the content of the photo is extremely important, we may call it *motivated.* That is, the importance of the photo is in the content, not in the form. As the content becomes less personally important as, for instance, in a portrait of an old man whom we don't know, or an abstract corporation logo, the sign becomes arbitrary. NBC, for instance, chose a new network logo a few years ago only to discover that it had been chosen independently by a public network in the middle west. The sign was not motivated by reference either to NBC or to Nebraska; it was an arbitrary sign.

Second and third order signification. When the content of a sign is motivated and iconic we call it a first-order sign. When a portrait of, say, a bicycle refers not to your specific bicycle but to the way in which a society uses bicycles it is a second-order sign. A second-order sign based on a bicycle may suggest fun, exercise or energy conservation. A second-order sign based on a picture of a house may mean security, family, or a substantial financial investment.

If the bicycle, as a signifier, is seen alongside other signifiers concerning heart disease, obesity and the pleasures of a vigorous life, we find that it has become a third-order signifier: it is part of a comprehensive sign system that describes the values and concerns of a society.

In the preceding chapter we dealt with myth criticism. Most myths are second-order signs. They have a significance more general than the interests of a single person, but may not be integrated in the overall sign system of a society. *One Day at a Time*, for instance, deals mythically with a woman seeking independence and successfully raising a family without an adult male. *Dallas*, on the other hand, emphasizes the way in which such micro-dramas are played out within the context of a rich family with a supporting local society that provides a complex web of supporting individuals. These competing myths (family vs. individual) are not integrated, in television, into a third-order comprehensive description of the society. Since television and radio programs deal, for the most part, with second-order signification, we have to look elsewhere for third-order signification. In the past, church provided such an integrating structure for many. We have come to expect presidents to achieve such integration as one aspect of their leadership. Lyndon Johnson, for instance, successfully integrated our consumer patterns into his "Great Society" legislation. John F. Kennedy successfully integrated his policies into the myth of an extended Cold War that would endure for generations. Gerald Ford failed to achieve third-order integration with his Whip Inflation Now (WIN) campaign, and President Carter's attempt to transform a high-consumption society into a lean, energy-conscious society succeeded only when it resorted to regulation, but failed to provide an integrated system of signs describing our society.

Television paradigms. The linguistic model provides one other pair of concepts which have value for the analysis of television and radio. A word in a sentence may function in two ways: syntagmatically and paradigmatically. In the following sentence, for instance, we can see the possible relations of the constituent words:

The boy tossed the ball to his father.

Below are listed words which could be substituted without doing violence to the "meaning" of the sentence:

The	boy	tossed the	ball	to his	father.
	girl	threw	apple	her	sister
	man	heaved	jacket		aunt
	child		book		uncle
	stranger				

The word *boy* is related syntagmatically to tossed, ball and father. That is, its relationship is determined by the structure of the sentence. The word *boy* is related paradigmatically to the words listed below it, since any of them could replace it without damaging the structure of the sentence (assuming the correct gender choice is made for the word *his*).

In film and television, individual visual "shots" function in a way loosely analagous to words. When a person in a picture smiles and points to a box, and the second picture is a close-up of a box of vitamin pills, we assume a syntagmatic relation between the smiling person and the box. The relation is syntagmatic. The box could be replaced with a picture of a football, a glass of beer, or a yo-yo. These three possible pictures have a paradigmatic relation.

Thus, a television picture of Walter Cronkite smiling (signifier) followed by a picture of an America's Cup sailboat (concept: American entry in international competition) makes an associative total that suggests American dominance in the yachting field. The picture of the sailboat could be replaced, paradigmatically, by pictures of little league ballplayers, a winning politician on election day, or any other appropriate phenomenon. The second-order myth would consequently vary with the paradigmatic change.

The linguistic origins of structuralist thinking have the advantages of providing an existing vocabulary, a conceptual scheme, and a wide-ranging literature. It has, however, one distinct disadvantage: we may assume that the analogy works more exactly than seems to be the case. For instance, if television pictures sometimes function like words, we may be led to assume that pictures are words, groups of pictures function like sentences, and that they are held together by a "grammar." Such pitfalls are characteristic of analogical thinking. We can avoid them by remembering that, although television may yield to structuralist inquiry based on the linguistic model, we have not yet found a visual "language." What we have found is associative groups that sometimes bear structural similarities to languages.

The Application to Television

In attempting this kind of analysis, it quickly becomes apparent that looking at one-hour programs in an attempt to identify overall structural patterns can be enormously time-consuming. More practice, in less time, can be had by beginning analyses of television and radio commercials. Most have some kind of narrative thread, and the attempt to take the product and make it part of an associative whole is almost universal.

For instance, I recently watched a commercial in which several athletes were interrupted while wearing the costumes appropriate for their sports. Each, by chance, was drinking orange juice. The *signifier* was the athlete with a glass of orange juice; the *signified* was the concept of health, activity and a natural drink appropriate for consumption after exercise. The *sign* is a society of healthful people who consume orange juice because, as Yvonne Goolagong said, "it's not just for breakfast anymore."

Automobile commercials have, depending upon the interests of consumers, associated cars with power, speed, fashion, convenience, fun and economy. One can easily identify the three basic units in the associative chain, and note the way in which sponsors create "new" commercials by making paradigmatic changes in old formats (for instance, Yvonne Goolagong may be replaced by a golfer, a baseball player, etc.).

Television news also provides productive territory for such inquiry. Raymond Williams, in *Technology and Cultural Form*, undertook an analysis of the rhythm and flow of television news. Early in 1978, Ms. Janet Meyer and I undertook an analysis of the narrative structures of television news. We attempted to identify the persons who were the actors in news stories, who was acted upon, the institutional affiliation of the actors, and the narrative in which the actors played out their drama.

We found that most actors were government officials, male, and that the most commonly acted-upon characters were also male government officials. The conflict, typically a struggle for power or an attempt to punish a villain, was equally predictable. The most common narrative, we found, was that of a struggle between government officials representing different commitments or constituencies. In the report, which appeared in the Spring, 1979, issue of the *Journal of Communication*, we emphasized the simplicity of the narratives and omitted the structuralist interpretation. The signifier was commonly the protagonist; the signified the concept of orderly and fair conflict resolution; the sign, the American government providing a forum for all viewpoints and a harmonious resolution in the public interest.

Television news, because of the large number of discrete narratives (news items) provides a rich source of materials for the structuralist.

Other Applications

The structuralist model can be applied not only to advertising and news programs, but to game shows and dramatic series as well. We began by pointing to *Vega$* as a program in which Tanna's relationship to his car, his side-kick, his secretary, the city of Las Vegas, the heroines and the villains all function as part of a second-order myth system in which Tanna and *Vega$* function as signifiers and a complex system of responsibility, compassion and corruption are signified. The sign is a society in which, even in a "wide open" city, enduring values operate.

Such analyses have not been undertaken on a large scale by American critics. It is a fruitful way of dealing with material which has not yielded to traditional criticism with its bias toward the excellent, the unique and the new. Television may find its fairest critics among the structuralists.

A Final Note

Geoffrey Hartman has noted that structuralism

> . . . is a complex and many-faceted intellectual movement: born in Russia and Switzerland, confirmed in Prague, sowing wild and fertile seed in France, but respecting the separation of disciplines and keeping to linguistics in America. It is not suited for monogamy, however. . . .[3]

At the moment structuralism is flirting with communication theory. The consequences of this intermingling are not easily predicted. At the moment, however, it provides one of the most exciting opportunities for critics interested in cutting new ground.

Notes

1. Terence Hawkes. *Structuralism and Semiotics* (Berkeley: University of California Press, 1976), p. 17.
2. Philip Pettit. *The Concept of Structuralism* (Berkeley: University of California Press, 1974), pp. 33-34.
3. Geoffrey Hartman. "Structuralism: The Anglo-American Adventure," in Ehrmann, Jacques. *Structuralism*. New York: Anchor Books, 1970, p. 137.

Suggested Readings

Chomsky, Noam. *Aspects of the Theory of Syntax*. Cambridge: MIT Press, 1965. The clearest argument that we "generate" new linguistic structures rather than learn them. The implications for those who favor a "visual language" are important.

Eco, Umberto. *A Theory of Signs*. Bloomington: Indiana University Press, 1979. A comprehensive outline of a science of signs. Eco, together with the American Thomas A. Sebeok, is one of the most prolific writers— and most influential—at the moment.

Eco, Umberto. *The Role of the Reader*. Bloomington: Indiana University Press, 1979. In this, Eco argues that "open" texts, such as *Finnegans Wake*, place different demands upon readers than "closed texts" such as detective stories.

Ehrmann, Jacques. *Structuralism*. New York: Anchor Books, 1970. One of the standard, and best, introductory readers.

Fiske, John and Hartley, John. *Reading Television*. London: Methuen & Co., 1978. An ambitious overview. One of the best applications of structuralism to television criticism.

Greenberg, Joseph H. *A New Invitation to Linguistics*. New York: Anchor Books, 1977. One of the best introductions to the language and thought of the field.

Hawkes, Terence. *Structuralism and Semiotics*. Berkeley: University of California Press, 1977. Like Pettit, a useful overview.

Kawin, Bruce F. *Telling It Again and Again*. Ithaca: Cornell University Press, 1972. A beguiling study of repetition and its uses in literature. The application to television, although not made by the author, is apparent.

Pettit, Philip. *The Concept of Structuralism*. Berkeley: University of California Press, 1977. If you have time for only one introductory reader, this is recommended.

Saussure, Ferdinand de. *Course in General Linguistics*. New York: McGraw-

Hill, 1966. Constructed from his lecture notes, this is the fountain from which structuralist and semiotic inquiry flows.

Sebeok, Thomas A. *Studies in Semiotics*. Bloomington: Indiana University Press, 1976. This and his later work, though difficult, provide the best index of American thinking.

Sebeok, Thomas A. *The Sign and Its Masters*. Austin: University of Texas Press, 1979. Readers will have to make the application to television, but the tools are presented here.

Public Policy and the Criticism of Broadcasting

We begin by noting that many critics grow weary of criticizing programs that are surprisingly similar in format, style, and content. One response to the sameness on the part of some critics has been to direct their critical poses toward two related questions: How did the system get this way? and What can be done about it? The search for answers to these questions leads them to examine the structure and functions of broadcasting. Although they may have numerous concerns, the ideas with which these critics are concerned are often grouped under the term "public policy."

Critics concerned with public policy need a broad knowledge of the regulatory agencies concerned with communication and a knowledge of the structure of the broadcasting industry and its related organizations—rating services, syndication houses, and news services. In short, they need a detailed knowledge of the industry so they can make judgments that are based upon sound understanding. Broadcasting operates in a political, social and economic environment. Those critics who choose to deal with these relationships, rather than program content, are somewhat political commentators.

It is obviously impossible to exhaust the concerns of such critics. In this section, we have chosen to deal with a number of issues which influence public policy in broadcasting, and we will attempt to define public policy in terms useful to critics. Throughout, the issues selected are representative and contemporary. They will date quickly, but the issues which they illustrate are likely to be with us for a longer period of time.

The Historical Moment

If we assume that public policy is merely the result of the competing interests of organized groups, it would be an inaccurate simplification. Public policy is influenced by the historical factors operating at the moment a policy determination is made. In the

1930s, Charlie McCarthy and his puppet master Edgar Bergen caused a stir by having a conversation with Mae West on network radio in which sexual suggestions were, very indirectly, made. Today, much more explicit sexual references are regularly tolerated. Subjects which were once considered taboo, such as drugs, abortion, and homosexuality, now are part of the arsenal of subjects with which a broadcaster may deal. The changes, in these instances, did not occur first in public policy. Rather, public policy followed after changes in society.

Instances of the influence of the historical moment are easy to find. The civil rights activities of the 1960s were reflected in the Federal Communications Commission (FCC) decision to require broadcasters to submit a report indicating the sex, race, and status of employees as an index of whether broadcasters are practicing fair employment. In a related field of social change, women began appearing as news reporters and in other roles formerly reserved for men at precisely the time when the women's movement was gaining national recognition and the Equal Rights Amendment was being debated.

Public policy in broadcasting is not merely an indication of the social mood or the political or economic climate. It is much too complex to respond to social change in a way that a barometer responds to air pressure. There is, however, a consistent drift in policies in the direction of the prevailing climate. The historical moment, though not decisive, is an important factor in the determination of public policy.

Public policy is influenced by a number of philosophic assumptions made by broadcasters, government regulators, and members of the general public. Many of these assumptions exist in the form of slogans, and it is to these shorthand designators that we direct our attention.

The Public Interest

When the Radio Act of 1927 was passed at the last moment before congressional adjournment, there was dissent within the house about the meaning of the phrase that radio should be regulated "in the public interest, convenience and necessity." Convenience and necessity have caused little difficulty, but the public interest has been a problem. The term, used earlier in legislation dealing with transportation, was sufficiently vague to encourage those in the Congress who favored governmental regulation of programming, while providing similar encouragement for those who felt that the new medium needed First Amendment protection as much as an orator or newspaper publisher. Thus, the public interest began in congressional debate and has continued to be debated by an ever-increasing number of persons for nearly fifty years.[1]

Several prominent ideas related to the public interest in broadcasting have developed. One point of view is that the public interest is *what the public is interested in listening to or viewing.* From this point of view, the audience ratings provide the best index. Those programs which attract the largest audiences are, by definition, holding the interest of the largest number or—to twist the meaning of the phrase slightly—serving the public interest. Broadcasters, for obvious reasons of self-interest, are prone to use this definition.

Others contend that the pressure to build large audiences results from advertising pressures, which distort programs by forcing producers to avoid controversial issues, experimental program forms, and the interests of minorities. They argue that some programs should be carried as "public service" or "sustaining" (that is, nonsponsored) programs. If programs were removed from the pressure to build large audiences, it is argued, they would improve qualitatively. This assumption was best argued in the "Memorandum on the Public Service Responsibility of Broadcast Licenses," popularly known as "The Blue Book," issued by the FCC in 1946.

This idea is currently being argued by those who favor the de-commercialization of children's programs. Unfortunately, the economics of broadcasting are such that unsponsored programs frequently are produced at minimum expense, resulting in poor quality. Professor William Melody has developed a unique proposal for replacing the advertising income for broadcasters with corporate foundation grants in the hope that the absence of advertiser pressure would provide freedom from violence in the programs, and that the presence of adequate funds would assure program quality. His book, *Children's Television: The Economics of Exploitation,* is a thorough development of this proposal.

A third argument is that the public interest is best served by offering "balanced" program schedules. "The Blue Book" contained recommendations that broadcasters carry a broad range of program types, including drama, local-live programs, talk shows, and news. The FCC allowed the number of radio stations to more than double in the decade following publication of "The Blue

Book," and the audience was consequently fragmented among many stations. In addition, the development of television in the early 1950s further reduced the available audience. As a result, radio stations were forced to specialize in specific formats: middle-of-the-road popular music (M.O.R.), country and western music, all news format, rock music, and classical music. The FCC even allowed one Los Angeles station to experiment with a want-ad format. Clearly, for radio at least, balance was not an economically viable concept.

Television stations, however, now have the public role formerly occupied by the major-market, network-affiliated radio stations in the 1940s. The FCC has made it clear that VHF stations, particularly, are expected to carry news programs, public affairs programs, religious programs, and programs which meet local community needs. The term "balance" is not heard very often these days, nor is it likely to be with cable systems making audience fragmentation likely in the future, but the concept remains interesting. Should each station carry a balance of various program types? If not, should each market achieve a balance by having stations specialize in specific program types or audiences?

Another prominent idea is that the public interest is best served by, or at least is concerned with, programs which are responsive to community needs. Historically, the FCC has had a vigorous interest in promoting local-live programming. It has attempted to require broadcasters to carry such programs and has looked with favor upon reports that broadcasters produced programs in consultation or cooperation with church groups, universities, or other non-profit organizations. In all programs, the broadcaster was the person who determined what problems would be considered and who would appear to deal with them.

In the 1960s, at a time of citizen activism on many issues, including civil rights for racial minorities and women, the Vietnam War, and consumer activism, the FCC proposed and later adopted a rule requiring licensees to conduct a survey of their communities, including interviews of both community leaders and the general citizenry. Broadcasters were then asked, when applying for a license renewal, to relate the results of their community survey to their programming. The aim was to make programs directly responsive to the felt needs of citizens. It was, and is, an attractive strategy. It allows the FCC to require programs which meet community needs without entering the forbidden territory of program regulation, and it provides a clear test of broadcaster responsiveness to the needs of the community. Although program decisions

remain the prerogative of the broadcaster, the community survey forces broadcasters to think about social context and, at
renewal time, to justify their decisions in terms of the needs of
the community.

Unfortunately, radio and television are two of the most important ways of communicating a sense of community problems
to the public. As a result, many surveys indicate that people consider their major problems to be those items which have already
been reported as problems. Thus, surveys seem to be a device
for reaffirming the decisions made by news directors. However,
those who defend the surveys point out that they force broadcasters to get to know their communities and that they make
community considerations more salient when program decisions
are made. Further, many stations have developed programs which
seek out listener opinion on community needs. Thus, the community survey may benefit the community in many informal ways,
even if the results of the survey contain little of surprise.

Cable television operators can be required to make provision
for public access and local educational programs. This suggests
that the concept of localism will be with us for some time to come.

Another prominent argument related to the public interest in
broadcasting—that some limitation on ownership of radio and television is in the public interest—has been put forth consistently
by the FCC. If the aim of regulatory policy is to achieve as nearly
a democratic distribution of facilities as possible, the FCC argues,
a one-station-per-owner policy would encourage the widest possible distribution of ownership. Such a policy would presumably
encourage the dissemination of a variety of viewpoints. It would
encourage ownership by members of minority groups with the con-
sequent possibility of minority-oriented programming. It would
prevent domination of the broadcasting industry by large corporations with the possibility of news manipulation and program
control which such domination implies. Clearly, in the most democratic of states, no one would own more than one station. In
the United States one owner may hold licenses for seven television
stations, five of which may be VHF, plus seven AM stations and
seven FM stations.

Unfortunately, the FCC, for a variety of reasons, has allowed
concentration of ownership to occur. In the 1930s, newspapers
were aggressive in applying for broadcast licenses. Many of them
had the financial strength to offer a strong program service and
facilities to offer local news. Further, many publishers were
politically influential. In numerous cases, the FCC decided that

the newspaper owner was the best available applicant. The consequence was that newspapers eventually owned more than 600 radio facilities. The Commission is now trying to eliminate cross-media ownership within a single market.

The early days of television presented the FCC with a similar problem. Television stations were expensive to build and were expected to show a financial loss for an unknown period. The FCC, eager to establish a strong national television service, frequently favored an applicant with a radio station because it was assured that the radio station would help support the television operation and that the owner's business acumen would provide the management needed to build the television service.

One of the most significant concentration-of-control cases in recent years concerned the proposed purchase of the American Broadcasting Corporation (ABC) television network and its owned and operated stations by International Telephone and Telegraph (ITT). ABC maintained that it needed the financial strength of a major corporation to compete successfully with the National Broadcasting Corporation (NBC) and Columbia Broadcasting System (CBS) networks. The FCC approved the merger in June 1967, but Department of Justice objections kept the issue before the courts. Eventually, on January 1, 1968, ITT withdrew from the hearing. The issue of concentration of control, in this instance, was pursued by the Department of Justice rather than the FCC.

The concentration-of-control issue was one of several concerned in the Boston WHDH case in which the Boston *Herald-Traveler* eventually lost its license in the longest administrative proceeding on record. In this bizarre case, the loss of the television station caused the newspaper to be sold to a competitor. Thus, an attempt to decrease concentration resulted in the loss of one community service.

We have not, of course, exhausted the list of assumptions behind regulatory attitudes toward the concept of the public interest, but the issues we have mentioned are fundamental. Clearly, there is room for heated conflict between those who argue for and against community surveys linked to programming. There is room also for differences of opinion between those who support the concept of one-license-to-a-customer and those who look for the best qualified, most experienced licensee. In short, the public interest should be considered a point of contact between competing interests rather than a static concept.

Social Responsibility

One of the terms which often enters discussions of public policy and broadcasting is "social responsibility." The term stems from the feudal notion that the enjoyment of wealth carries with it public responsibilities. Some nineteenth-century barons, notably Carnegie, paid homage to the concept, while Ford and Rockefeller discovered the delights of philanthropy somewhat later. In our time the term has been applied to corporations rather than individuals, and considerable confusion has resulted.

The term has proven useful for citizen groups that wish to make a demand upon a broadcaster. Since a "responsibility" as general as this has no precise limits, it is possible that a demand of any sort (news of specific interest groups, less advertising, carrying a special show, etc.) might fall within it. The term is also useful for broadcasters who may wish to place decisions or activities in a most favorable light. To the extent that they can identify their activities with the concept, they can argue against regulatory activities by the FCC.

The term came into public discussion during the ferment which followed World War II. At the University of Chicago, the Commission on the Freedom of the Press argued that nonregulatory reinforcement of the concept of social responsibility would invigorate the American press. Broadcasting has, since its inception, been less free and more susceptible to advertising, public, and governmental pressures than the press; but many hoped that the spirit of the commission would encourage open discussion on radio and, eventually, television.

For broadcasters, social responsibility has a particularly potent ring, because they occupy a scarce resource. With only twelve VHF channels, augmented by numerous but little-used UHF channels, the television broadcaster on a VHF channel has a prize with the value of, perhaps, a crown patent three centuries ago. With privilege, some say, should go responsibility.

The concept of social responsibility is best understood in terms of competing concepts. Siebert, Peterson, and Schramm[2] argue that the social responsibility theory is a development of the libertarian theory championed by John Stuart Mill in the nineteenth century. Mill argued that a marketplace of ideas existed in which ideas, like products, competed for consumer attention. The best would survive the competition, he argued, and the shortcomings of the others would be revealed. Even as Mill argued for the marketplace, newspapers in urban centers were developing a concentration of control of ideas and information that made it clear that the marketplace could be distorted if one of the ideas was backed by a monopoly newspaper.

In broadcasting the marketplace was never open. Although all citizens could theoretically print their opinions and distribute them as broadsides at very low cost, they could not operate a radio or television station without government approval. Frustrating attempts at nongovernmental reform led numerous groups to seek regulatory solutions to what they felt were failures to keep the marketplace open. Other groups, supporting social responsibility theory, argued that, although government control was one way of rectifying marketplace failures (Siebert describes authoritarian and communist models), the marketplace could be opened without resorting to such control. Instead, control would be exercised by managers who would respond to "professional ethics" and public opinion.

Because of their favored position in the marketplace of ideas, broadcasters have a vital responsibility for insuring that "everyone who has something to say" is heard. The idea comes alive, however, only when applied to a specific situation: Was a broadcaster fair in reporting issues in your community? Did opposing views have an opportunity to be heard? If not, how can you, as a viewer or listener, enlarge the marketplace?

Regulation

The advocates of a free (unregulated) market system assume that the forces of supply and demand will determine the optimum distribution of goods and services without any interference (regulation) by government. The Invisible Hand of the marketplace, they argue, is both more effective and less onerous than the clumsy regulatory efforts of Big Brother. In the late nineteenth-century, however, the marketplace of goods and services as well as the "marketplace of ideas" failed. Railroad owners and oil distributors worked in concert to control the market and stifle competition. Newspapers and a few publishing houses enjoyed similar control of the goods by which ideas were exchanged.

In an attempt to correct the economic marketplace, Congress passed the Sherman Antitrust Act and, to make it effective, created the Interstate Commerce Commission. The concern with failures of the free market led to the creation of other regulatory agencies, including, in 1929, the Federal Radio Commission. This commission was succeeded in 1934 by the new Federal Communications Commission, which was given control of land-line communication as well as radio. The FCC was given authority to issue three-year (now five-year) licenses, to set technical standards, and, most important, to make judgments about who should get licenses.

The FCC has gradually expanded its powers by litigation but has never entered the field of program regulation, except indirectly. It has, for instance, described program types it found desirable, and it has been concerned with ownership patterns, lotteries, obscenity, hiring practices, and network affiliate relations. It has not, however, entered two fields: rate-setting and the prior restraint of programs.

Issues before the FCC change from time to time, but a number have been continuing concerns: concentration of control; network domination of evening programming; the political uses of broadcasting; fairness in treatment of controversial issues; advertising excesses; concern for children's programming; amounts of program time devoted to news, religion, and local programs; and citizen access to the media.

In criticizing the judgments of the FCC or theorizing about policies, it may be well to consider the unwieldly nature of American broadcasting and the complexity of making policy determinations. Five cases will be cited: the Fairness Doctrine, the Prime-Time Access Rule, self-regulation as demonstrated by family viewing time, public broadcasting, and the activities of citizen groups.

The Fairness Doctrine and personal attack rules. In 1949 the FCC issued a Report on Editorializing by Broadcast Licensees which ruled that broadcasters could editorialize as long as they presented other points of view. Ten years later the FCC enacted the "equal opportunities" rule which required broadcasters to present programming on controversial issues and provide fair coverage, including right of reply. The licensee retained the authority to determine which issues should be included in programming, as well as the right to select representative speakers for opposing views. There is an interesting possibility under this rule, however, that a broadcaster may inadvertently touch on an issue and fall within the Fairness Doctrine obligation requirement to provide right of reply.

Such an issue was inadvertently triggered by cigarette advertising, which was ruled by the courts, against FCC objections, to be "controversial." The result was the series of anti-smoking announcements which appeared on television. This case was later cited by consumer groups and environmentalists who argued that oil and power companies were buying time for commercials that raised controversial issues.

The critic considering this issue needs to make a difficult decision between the well-being of the marketplace of ideas and the extent to which broadcasters are exploited by those seeking to promote their views. The impetus to open access to the media has come primarily from the Department of Justice rather than from the FCC. Critics may wish to consider whether the problem, so far, has been exploitation or temerity.

Perhaps the most famous Fairness Doctrine case is the Red Lion, Pennsylvania, case, in which WGCB challenged the right of writer Fred Cook to have time to reply to criticism of his broadcast on the station. In a crucial decision for those who favor the Fairness Doctrine, the Supreme Court upheld the FCC's decision that Cook was entitled to time for reply.

The case established the legal solidity of the Doctrine and served as an example of how the free marketplace of ideas could be preserved. Or did it? In the *New York Times*, March 30, 1975, Fred Friendly argued that Cook asked for air time at the behest of the Democratic National Committee, which was concerned about right-wing political broadcasts. Was the marketplace of ideas maintained against the rights of the incumbent licensee, or was it subtly rigged so that access became a political weapon? The critic has a difficult decision to make.

The prime-time access rule. One of the most interesting experiments in regulation to occur in recent years has been the FCC's attempt to limit network domination of prime-time evening hours. In March 1965 the FCC introduced a "50-50 plan" which precluded the networks from owning or controlling more than 50 percent of the programs scheduled during prime-time viewing hours. It was hoped that this would encourage independent (non-network) producers to enter into the production of prime-time programs. After extensive hearings, in which the networks and economists opposed the plan, the FCC abandoned its proposal in favor of a "prime-time access rule" proposed by the Westinghouse Broadcasting Company.

The plan, announced in 1970, (1) prohibited stations in the top 50 markets containing at least three stations from taking more than three hours of network programming, other than news, between 7 and 11 p.m.; (2) prohibited networks from owning or controlling more than 50 percent of their prime-time entertainment programming; and (3) prohibited networks from engaging in domestic syndication (off-network sale) of their programs or acquiring subsidiary rights in the independently produced programs that they air.

The plan won approval from the ABC network because it eased their financial burdens by requiring one hour less of programming per night. The other networks objected. Westinghouse, which hoped to produce some programs for the non-network prime-time hours, supported the plan vigorously. Independent producers and others were mixed in their reactions to the plan.

The plan went into effect in the autumn of 1971. In January 1974 the FCC revised the rule, returning Sunday evenings to the networks and one-half hour on weekdays. The revised plan went into effect in September 1974.

The result of the rule is difficult to evaluate. Independent producers did enter the field of prime-time programming, but most of the programs accepted by broadcasters were game shows. Quiz shows were particularly popular because of their low production cost. An analysis of the programs appearing in your community in the early evening, post-news time will indicate whether the rule has had beneficial effects.

Self-regulation. If the marketplace is biased by a shortage of channels and the dominance of a few broadcasters, and if regulatory efforts lead to Byzantine complexities, where can a critic look for alternatives? One solution which broadcasters find attractive is the notion of self-regulation.

Self-regulation is a notion derived from the systems for the maintenance of standards devised by the medical and legal professions. In both, unlike broadcasting, admission to the profession is controlled by the members of the profession. Practitioners can be expelled by a group of peers without recourse to the courts. Both medicine and law are practiced on a small scale, by an individual or small group. Individuals can be easily controlled by these professional associations, which can not only use economic sanctions (appointments to hospitals, referrals, etc.) but also withdraw accreditation, eliminating a member from the profession.

Can an association of corporations, in broadcasting, electronics, or construction, be comparably "self-regulating"? There have been numerous attempts. In 1923 the American Society of Newspaper Editors adopted the "Canons of Journalism," which concerned the public's right to know, rather than standards of journalistic integrity. The National Association of Broadcasters created their "Code of Ethics" in 1929 in response to the Federal Radio Commission's interest in program content.

Revised periodically, the code for television is enforced by a broadcast-board whose sole authority is to remove the code seal from member stations. There are no economic sanctions, and the code authority cannot drum a broadcaster out of the business. The present code is available from the National Association of Broadcasters on inquiry and provides an interesting basis for criticism of the industry.

Self-regulation usually results from external pressure, has limited enforcement provisions, complies with economic realities, and is useful primarily for opposing external regulation. Clearly, such corporate self-regulation is different from and less effective than that exercised by the law and medical professions whose codes served as models.

Critics may have a difficult time supporting self-regulation, but they may nevertheless find it attractive if other regulatory schemes seem even less effective.

Public broadcasting. One of the most interesting problems for the critic interested in public policy is public broadcasting. An outgrowth of a small number of radio stations supported, for the most part, by educational institutions and by means other than the sales of commercials, public radio stations had no formal place in American broadcasting until 20 FM stations were reserved for noncommercial use in 1945 and 242 television channels were reserved by the Sixth Report and Order in 1952.

Even when channels were reserved, the growth of public broadcasting was slow because of the lack of funds. In 1967 the report of the Carnegie Commission (which suggested the term "public broadcasting" rather than "educational") served as a model for federal legislation which created the Corporation for Public Broadcasting. The corporation funnels federal funds to individual stations but does not participate in the production of programs. Program decisions are made by member stations of the Public Broadcasting Service through a Byzantine voting procedure.

If the organization of the service is fluid, its problems are remarkably consistent. The first, by any reckoning, is the problem of paying for the system. Federal financing has been resisted by Congress because of a fear that federal control of programming may accompany the funds. Taxes on the sale of sets, earmarked for public broadcasting, have been considered a potential non-political source, but manufacturers have resisted anything which might raise the cost of their products. States and municipalities find it hard to justify large-scale support of stations. The problem is nagging and crucial, but no workable solution is in sight.

Other problems for the critic interested in public broadcasting can be quickly summarized:

1. Should program production be centralized to achieve higher quality and production efficiencies? Or should local stations continue to play a role, encouraging the growth of strong regional stations and the programming which stems from their unique resources? Some of the strongest public stations are located in Boston, San Francisco, Pittsburgh, New York and Washington.

2. Should public stations strive to achieve quality programs at the expense of large audiences? Or should a larger audience be cultivated to provide a base of public support for the system? Or should the needs of special interest groups be met at the expense of both excellence and audience size? This problem of priorities remains unresolved, and many stations are attempting to accomplish all three, simultaneously.

3. Should there be a "live" public network comparable to the three commercial networks, or should scheduling options be left to individual stations with only special events carried on a network basis? The rapid growth and acceptance of National Public Radio (NPR) and the Public Broadcasting Service (PBS) in television suggest that, with the aid of satellite interconnection, live networking of a flexible kind is in the near future.

4. Should public television cultivate its own production facilities and staffs (responsible for such programs as "French Chef") or purchase programs from independent producers such as Children's Television Workshop ("Sesame Street")? The central question is: should public television become a major program producer, such as the BBC or the Hollywood program producers, or should it become a program brokerage?

5. Should public broadcasting be concerned with news and public affairs broadcasting? Opponents have argued that

public broadcasting, free from pressures of the audience and dependent on government funding, may become a propaganda medium. Exponents argue that a concern with ratings and acceptability prevents commercial broadcasters from use of hard-hitting investigative journalism and frank discussions of public issues. Only public broadcasting, they argue, can right the imbalance and conservatism of the commercial broadcasters. The *Mac-Neil/Lehrer Report* is an example of what public broadcasting can do in the public affairs field.

6. Is a new organizational structure needed to make public broadcasting more efficient and more effective? If so, how would it be organized?

None of the questions listed above is susceptible to a two-value, yes-or-no solution. All require compromise and the balancing of conflicting interests. The critic can contribute by making public and comprehensible a debate that is often concealed from the public's scrutiny.

Citizen-action groups. Broadcasting has had citizen groups to contend with since the early 1930s. It was not until the 1960s, however, that such groups had legal standing before the FCC.

The WLBT case, Jackson, Mississippi, is a landmark in the evolution of citizen intervention in broadcasting. In 1966 the United Church of Christ, together with two leaders of the Jackson black community, filed a petition to deny the renewal of the station's license. When the FCC denied them "standing" to participate in the hearings as parties, they went to the District of Columbia U.S. Court of Appeals and were granted standing.

Since that time numerous groups have formed to participate in hearings and to provide counsel to local citizens. Some, including the two best known, the Citizens Communication Center and the National Citizens Committee for Broadcasting (NCCB), are located in Washington. Others, such as the National Association for Better Broadcasting (California) and the American Council for Better Broadcasts, Inc. (Wisconsin), have regional identities. Still others, such as Action for Children's Television (ACT) and the National Latino Media Coalition, are concerned with the interests of specialized groups. The addresses of these and other organizations will be found in the *Aspen Handbook*, which is listed at the end of this chapter.

It is difficult to estimate the effectiveness of these groups. Working as pressure groups, they frequently ask for more change than eventually occurs. In many areas of broadcasting, however, change has occurred at a faster pace than in past years. There is less violence in children's programs, there are more minority group members and women on the screen, and minority groups have more responsible jobs than in the past. In short, it is likely that, without citizen-action groups, broadcasting would not be as responsive to social change.

A variety of guides for those who wish to influence public policy—or simply reform a local broadcaster—are available. Some are listed at the end of this chapter.

The Current Situation

During 1978 and 1979 critics of broadcasting watched with great interest as two quite different groups began making plans for the future of American broadcasting. In the House of Representatives, Congressman Lionel Van Deerlin chaired a Subcommittee charged with rewriting the Communications Act of 1934. The attempt to simplify and rationalize the much-revised Act seemed to get off to a promising start. The Subcommittee staff, young, eager and well-trained, arranged extensive hearings and produced a number of position papers which concisely indicated the kinds of changes needed: the deregulation of radio; planning for the growth of cable television; an innovative proposal to auction television channels and to simplify reports to federal agencies.

Simultaneously, the Carnegie Foundation, for the second time, formed a Commission to look into the well-being of public broadcasting. Aware that there was conflict between local managers who cherished their autonomy and those attempting to establish a national program service, as well as confusion about the role of federal funding in public broadcasting, the staff of Carnegie II held hearings and considered alternative proposals. Theirs was a heavy burden because the first Carnegie Report (in which the term "public broadcasting" was suggested to replace "educational broadcasting") had been instrumental in bringing significant change to the public broadcasting industry.

The promise of the reports was not fulfilled. Early in 1979 the

Carnegie Commission report was issued. It suggested modest changes in the structure of the Corporation for Public Broadcasting, more autonomy for the Public Broadcasting Service, and stability of federal support. It was well argued, but it did not galvanize informed opinion in the same way as Carnegie I.

Late in 1979 the House Subcommittee report was rejected by the Committee from which it stemmed. The Subcommittee staff has continued to explore satellite, cable, and other policy problems, but the initial promise of a radical restructuring of broadcast regulation has not occurred.

The reasons for the failure of these groups to live up to their promise may be placed on their staffs, leadership, or on the political promise. It is possible that they failed, however, because the problems they dealt with were being overwhelmed by new developments in technology which made some of the older policy problems obsolete.

Meanwhile, the FCC continues to regulate on the basis of the Communications Act of 1934. It regulates with occasionally surprising vigor. As this book is prepared for press, the FCC has announced that it will withdraw licenses for three VHF television stations owned by RKO General, Inc.: WNAC—TV, Boston; WOR—TV, New York; and WHJ—TV, Los Angeles. The decision, by a narrow 4-3 vote will no doubt be appealed. No matter what the outcome of the appeal, however, the importance of the case for the critic is clear: the FCC is continuing to innovate in its efforts to serve the public interest.

In the RKO General case, the decision was based upon an investigation of the corporation by the Securities and Exchange Commission. A subsidiary of the General Tire and Rubber Co., with the same person acting as chairman of the board of both corporations, RKO General was found to be insufficiently insulated from the problems of its mother corporation. The issue? The SEC charged that General Tire was guilty of foreign tax evasion, falsification of stockholder reports, filing false reports, and bribing foreign agents and officials. The Commission said the nature and scope of the misconduct by RKO and its parent corporation, General Tire, was so extensive and serious and so unlike any other situation, that the FCC "could not be assured that RKO could be trusted in the future to operate in a manner consistent with FCC standards."

And so we find ourselves in an unexpected situation. Instead of having leadership provided by the Congress in the form of new legislation, or from private foundation task forces, we find that the FCC, implementing the nearly half-century old 1934 legislation, is once again the focus of policy formulation.

Public Policy Is . . .

Public policy is the accretion of decisions on specific issues over a period of time. It is influenced by the historical moment, by regulation—both governmental and industrial—by citizen groups, by technological change (the decision to establish UHF and FM channels was made by the FCC, but it depended upon technological development), and by political factors stemming from the White House (FCC commissioners are nominated by the president, confirmed by the Senate) and Congress (Congress both berates the industry and provides protection whenever it is threatened). The complexity of the preceding sentence may serve as a model for the process of determining public policy.

The FCC has been criticized for its lack of long-range planning, and it was hoped that the creation of an Office of Telecommunications Planning in the executive branch would provide rational policy guidance in the field of communications. To date, however, policy has continued to be the sum of influence distorted by historical accidents. Perhaps this is consistent with the American distrust of centralized planning.

The idea that competition among differing interests will serve the public interest has recently been challenged. John Gardner, whose Common Cause organization has achieved considerable notoriety, has commented that such conflict has not solved social problems in the past. Others have expressed the conviction that "the person who claims to serve the community interest is a power grabber." Perhaps a difference exists between those who work to define the public interest and those who actively seek to exercise power in what they conceive to be the public interest. Although special interests may benefit temporarily from exploiting the term, no society is likely to function, as Irving Kristol has said, "without some notion of what the public interest is."

Critics who wish to deal with these issues are committing themselves to an extensive background research project. None of the issues is simple, many of them inter-connect, and there is no sense of direction to guide those concerned with them. Perhaps in this field the person who considers the issues from the point of view of the audience—without special interest group limitations—may have a contribution to make to our understanding of broadcasting.

Notes

1. For a sense of how the term is being used currently, there is no better source than the journal, *The Public Interest,* edited by Irving Kristol. For its specific application to broadcasting, *Broadcasting Magazine,* a trade weekly, provides ready access to current thinking by broadcasters and their critics.

2. See Fred Siebert, et al., *Four Theories of the Press: The Authoritarian, Libertarian, Social Responsibility, and Soviet Communist Concepts of What the Press Can Be and Do* (Urbana: University of Illinois Press, 1963).

Suggested Readings

Philosophic Assumptions

Chaffee, Zachariah, Jr. *Government and Mass Communications.* Chicago: University of Chicago Press, 1947. Two volumes. A broader consideration of the philosophic assumptions about mass communication.

Laski, Harold J. *The Rise of European Liberalism.* London: G. Allen and Unwin Ltd., 1936. The classic analysis of the rise of the ideas which favor non-governmental liberal pressure on the press.

Head, Sydney W. *Broadcasting in America.* Boston: Houghton Mifflin Company, 1975. The best single-volume overview of American Broadcasting. Contains background on the issues mentioned here, cable television, public broadcasting, and social effects.

Schubert, Glendon. *The Public Interest.* New York: The Free Press, 1960. A summary of the background and factors which led to the formulation of the concept of a public interest.

Social Responsibility

Commission on Freedom of the Press. *A Free and Responsible Press.* Chicago: University of Chicago Press, 1947. An attempt to reform the press without recourse to economic or regulatory punishment.

Rivers, William L., and Wilbur Schramm. *Responsibility in Mass Communication.* Rev. ed. New York: Harper and Row, 1969. A thorough overview of the issues.

Siebert, Fred S., Theodore Peterson, and Wilbur Schramm. *Four Theories of the Press.* Urbana: University of Illinois Press, 1963. An excellent basic discussion of the origins of our notions of a marketplace of ideas and the usefulness of social responsibility as a policy.

Smith, Robert R. "Social Responsibility: A Term We Can Do Without." In *Corporate Social Policy,* edited by Robert L. Heilbroner and Paul London. Reading, Massachusetts: Addison Wesley, 1975. An argument that the term is applied so indiscriminately that it has lost its usefulness.

Regulation

Carnegie Commission on Educational Television. *Public Television: A Pro-*

gram for Action. New York: 1967. The document provided a model for the Public Broadcasting Act of 1967.

Clark, David, and Earl R. Hutchinson. *Mass Media and the Law: Freedom and Restraint.* New York: Wiley-Interscience, 1970. A useful summary that is wider in scope than those concerned solely with broadcasting.

A Public Trust: The Report of the Carnegie Commission on the Future of Public Broadcasting. New York: Bantam Books, 1979. The second Carnegie Report. It raises the current issues, suggests organizational solutions.

Cole, Barry, and Mal Oettinger. *Reluctant Regulators: The FCC and the Broadcasting Audience.* Reading, Mass.: Addison-Wesley, 1978. An "inside" analysis of the Commission's workings, with unique information about the license renewal process.

Friendly, Fred. *The Good Guys, the Bad Guys, and the First Amendment.* New York: Random House, 1976. A re-examination of an historic case which demonstrates how the regulatory process can be put in the service of special interests.

Gillmor, Donald M., and Jerome A. Barron. *Mass Communication Law.* St. Paul, Minnesota: West Publishing Company, 1969. A valuable handbook with periodic supplements.

Kahn, Frank J. *Documents of American Broadcasting.* New York: Appleton-Century-Crofts, 1974. The starting point for discussions of policy. Includes excerpts from laws, rules and regulations, decisions, and court decisions.

Kohlmeier, Louis M., Jr. *The Regulators.* New York: Harper and Row, 1969. A readable overview by a veteran journalist. Only one chapter is devoted specifically to broadcasting.

Krasnow, Erwin G., and Lawrence D. Longley. *The Politics of Broadcast Regulation.* (2d ed.). New York: St. Martin's Press, 1978. Less jaded than the title suggests, the book provides a worldly overview of the process of regulation.

Levin, Harvey J. *Broadcast Regulation and Joint Ownership of Media.* New York: New York University Press, 1960. A thorough statement of the difficulties underlying the concentration-of-control issue.

Melody, William. *Children's Television: The Economics of Exploitation.* New Haven, Connecticut: Yale University Press, 1973. An attempt to free children's programs from advertiser pressure by finding alternative funding.

Noll, Roger G., Merton J. Peck, and John J. McGowan. *Economic Aspects of Television Regulation.* Washington, D.C.: The Brookings Institution, 1974. They argue that the FCC has served the interests of broadcasters by protecting them from competition. A serious and well-supported indictment of the current regulatory system.

Robinson, Glen O., ed. *Communications for Tomorrow: Policy Perspectives for the 1980's.* New York: Praeger Special Studies, 1978. A broad view of how technological changes will affect public policy.

Siepmann, Charles. *Radio's Second Chance.* Boston: Little, Brown and Company, 1946. Appearing at the same time as the FCC's "Blue Book," this volume argued that FM made possible many of the goals. A much neglected general statement of a possible public policy.

Self-Regulation

Hellfrich, Stockton. "The Radio and Television Codes and the Public Interest." *Journal of Broadcasting* (Summer, 1970): 267-274. A man who has administered the code argues that it serves the public.

National Association of Broadcasters. "The Television Code of the National Association of Broadcasters." Washington, D.C. Revised Periodically. See also the Code of the Radio and Television News Directors Association (listed in the *Aspen Handbook on the Media*).

Citizen-Action Groups

Bennet, Robert W. *A Lawyer's Source Book: Representing the Audience in Broadcasting Proceedings.* New York: Office of Communications, United Church of Christ, 1974. A how-to book for attorneys representing citizen groups written in generally accessible terms.

Johnson, Nicholas. *How to Talk Back to Your Television Set.* Boston: Little, Brown and Company, 1970. Also Bantam paperback, 1970. Former FCC commissioner gives advice to citizens.

Kaye, Evelyn. *The Family Guide to Children's Television.* New York: Pantheon Books, 1974. Much useful information for citizen groups, not limited in application to children's programs.

Rivers, William L., and William T. Slater, eds. *Aspen Handbook on the Media.* 1975-76 Edition. Palo Alto, California: Aspen Institute Program on Communications and Society, 1975. The single most useful source for a student concerned with public policy and broadcasting. The index of organizations lists all those mentioned in this text.

The Criteria for Evaluating Broadcasting

There are no widely agreed upon coordinating principles in broadcasting criticism. Some critics transfer criteria from journalism when evaluating news programs, or from theatre when evaluating television drama. Others apply standards taken from politics. Since the criteria vary, we will not recommend specific criteria which we feel are appropriate for criticizing broadcasting. Rather, we have assembled an outline of criteria which others have found useful and which may be applied to programs. The categories are neither exhaustive nor mutually exclusive; rather, they are a series of starting points for broadcast criticism.

1. *Genre*. It may be useful to assign a program to its genre and apply the standards which have proven appropriate for dealing with other programs of the same kind.

   a. News.

      Does the reporter compensate for his or her biases?
      Is the report as complete as possible?
      Are important details overlooked?
      Is the reporting balanced or one-sided?
      Do the visuals enhance or interfere with a comprehension of the event?
      Are the events selected for inclusion significant?

   b. Detective-adventure.

      Does the program have a unique quality?
      Is it stylistically consistent?
      Does the viewer find it easy to suspend disbelief while watching or listening?
      Does the denouement relate to the body of the program?
      Does the program vary from episode to episode, or is it repetitious?

   c. Situation comedy.

      How is this program different from other programs of this type?

Does it reflect problems of interest to the audience?
Are the solutions to problems plausible?
Does it derive from other, similar programs?

d. Sports.

Is the reporting fair or does the reporter support one team or contender?
Are the possibilities of the medium—instant replay, special effects, etc.—exploited?
Are the camera shots, language, or analysis original or repetitious?
Does the broadcast help the viewer understand why events occur in the sport, or does it merely report what happens?
Is the game changed in any way to simplify television coverage (for instance, by inserting time-outs for commercials or by introducing sudden-death endings so that the duration of a game can be predicted)?

e. Variety programs.

Do the component parts of the show fit together cohesively?
Is the program distinctive from other shows of the type?
Does the pacing of the program hold the viewer's interest?
Does the program take advantage of the potential of the medium used, or is it a theatre presentation simply being broadcast?
Does the program have variety or sameness?

f. Documentaries.

Is the research for the program original or derived from some secondary source, acknowledged or unacknowledged?
Does the program have shape in that the component parts lead to the conclusion?
Does the program appear to be produced as a documentary or assembled from bits and pieces left over from news and other programs?
Do the producers make their biases clear or do they imply that they are disinterested?
Are the producers biased?
Could the program have been done as well in some other medium, for instance, a newspaper or magazine?
Do the producers lean heavily on interviews?

g. Game shows.

Is the show in some way unique?

Are the prizes of real value or—as in "What's My Line"—
are they party prizes of little value?

Are the contestants presented sympathetically or exploited?

Do the audience responses seem appropriate or do they
appear to be "hyped"?

What motivates the contestants?

Is the program concerned with fun, competition, or greed?

h. Interviews.

Is the interviewer prepared with background material and
questions which provoke interesting answers?

Does the person being interviewed have an opportunity to
present his or her point of view?

Does the interviewer probe for clarification of answers?

Are the questions about important matters?

Is too much time spent on trivia?

Could other questions, or questions asked differently, have
elicited more interesting responses?

Obviously, each genre—western, instructional, etc.—suggests
criteria which are appropriate to programs of that type. Each
individual program will suggest additional questions appropriate to it. For the critic, the important act is the one of
categorizing, of assigning each program to its genre and
evaluating it in terms appropriate to it.

2. *Innovation.* In nearly all genre, innovation is a quality re-
spected by both critics and viewers. Innovation may be a
matter of using a person of the opposite sex in a familiar
role, as in "Police Woman," a hero with an unusual handicap,
as in "Ironside," or a host who is quieter and more thoughtful
than others in similar roles, as is Dick Cavett. Wherever
innovation occurs, it is the job of the critic to evaluate its
contribution to the program.

3. *Use of the Medium.* A rewarding question for the critic is,
Does a specific program make the most of the possibilities
inherent in the medium? Comedian Ernie Kovacs was widely
acclaimed for being one of the few performers to use the
visual aspect of television for comic effects. The producers
of network television football and baseball coverage have
exploited the visual possibilities of the medium, as an after-
noon spent watching either of these sports on television will
reveal. Radio has its own unique possibilities. Disc jockeys
have explored the possibility of creating a close personal
bond with listeners. Radio equipment can be moved to

nearly any location quickly and cheaply; helicopter traffic reports and on-the-spot news coverage exploit radio's portability. And, of course, radio is extremely portable for listeners, who can carry it with them on boats, in cars, and on beaches.

4. *Public Needs*. Broadcasting has a responsibility to meet the needs of the public it serves for entertainment, information, and enlightenment. Public needs are not easily determined. Occasionally, public officials or editors speak out about needs and priorities. Sometimes, pressure groups will make their preferences known. Most of the time, however, the critic must make the complicated determination about the relation of broadcasts to public goals and the needs of the various audiences served by broadcasting. The critic may ask:

Is a program consistent with FCC rules and regulations?
Does a program further or otherwise relate to the public goals of the country on such matters as racial integration, energy conservation, or participation in political decisions?
Are groups in the community with specific needs represented in the broadcasts available in their area?
Do programs address the problems faced by local communities and the nation?

5. *Effects*. Many critics judge programs by their presumed effects. If a program contains violence, it may be presumed by some to encourage violent behavior. If it demonstrates effective community action to solve a problem, it may encourage similar behavior in the communities where the program is listened to or viewed. Most critics concerned with effects, as we will see in the second section of this book, are concerned with whether a specific program is likely to have pro-social effects (learning constructive behaviors) or whether the program might possibly contribute to the continuation of social problems. Critics concerned with effects may ask:

Does a program contain substantial violence?
Does a program demonstrate conflict or cooperation?
Does a program encourage trust or suspicion?
Are the characters in a program useful as role models?
Are the solutions to problems demonstrated in programs potentially useful in everyday life?

6. *Taste*. Most informal television and radio criticism is based on taste. Viewers "like" or "don't like" programs according to their own opinions. The Romans perhaps said all that can be said: *De gustibus non disputandem est.*

Yet, it may be useful for a critic to convert expressions of taste into other terms. For instance, protests about excess numbers of commercials may be related to specific quantities of time. If the critic can determine how many minutes per hour creates the feeling of "excess," it becomes possible to discuss with some objectivity what otherwise remains a subjective judgment.

Taste is a particularly important matter in discussing television, because those who like it least—upper income and educated families—are also likely to be least represented in the audience. Taste needs to be related to social class and to viewing habits if it is to be of use in evaluating television.

It might be argued that the aim of criticism is to develop taste on the part of both critic and audience by consciously addressing the many factors involved in making a qualitative judgment. Perhaps there is no arguing with taste, but the development of it may be the ultimate aim of criticism.[1]

Note

1. Although there is little agreement upon these categories, one of the most extensive lists will be found in *The Rhetoric of Television* by Ronald Primeau (New York: Longman, Inc., 1979). The book is a mixture of sound specifics about television and theoretical explanations. In the form of a workbook, the lists and worksheets are useful and may stimulate readers to devise their own.

II Issues in Broadcast Criticism

Although critics are concerned with a wide range of issues, some are more pressing and others more enduring than most. In this section, we have selected two "evergreen" issues: broadcast journalism and the social effects of broadcasting. We have also added one issue of pressing importance: the role of cable television and the new distribution systems which promise to change broadcasting as we have known it.

Broadcast Journalism

Richard Nixon, Lyndon Johnson and Jimmy Carter might all agree on one thing: each felt that television news treated him shabbily while he was in the White House. And so while broadcasters think of television news as one of the most expensive and most profitable aspects of their business, critics are likely to think of it as one of the most controversial.

News broadcasts on radio began in controversy. Newspapers, fearing competition from the new medium, attempted to hamper the development of radio news. They opposed the use of wire services by radio; they threatened prosecution for plagiarism if radio newscasters "borrowed" from newspapers; and, to complicate matters, many newspapers constructed or purchased radio stations to protect themselves. The criticism of radio news was, in some ways, a simple matter. Since it consisted of words read aloud, the material read could be compared with the news printed in newspapers. Because newspapers usually contained more words, radio news was often thought to be inferior.

Radio provided two additions to the news gathering methods of the newspaper. The first, the commentator, was born of the need to program news at a time when the networks did not have adequate independent news services. The commentators—Raymond Swing, Gabriel Heatter, Lowell Thomas, H. V. Kaltenborn, Fulton Lewis, Jr., and many others—provided radio with a unique service: an analysis of the day's events dramatized by the personality of the commentator. Even if radio news services were inferior to the wire services and the leading newspapers, commentary was an innovation that could not be matched by print journalists.

The second contribution made by radio was "on-the-spot" reporting from the field. The Spanish Civil War, the Hindenberg disaster, sports events, and political conventions were brought "live" into the homes of millions. Although we are now aware of the many editorial decisions that were made in each broadcast, radio at the time seemed to many to take audiences into the field and give them a first-hand experience of world events. Perhaps the most famous and most readily available on recordings were the broadcasts from London by Edward R. Murrow, which began, "This is London . . . ."

Radio broadcasters were not universally admired. The easy familiarity with the rich and famous affected by some broadcasters and their attractive voices led critics to suspect that there was less to their reports than met the ear. John P. Marquand, in *So Little Time*, wrote about Walter Newcombe, a radio journalist who specialized in pompous, empty analyses and name-dropping. The novel is an interesting depiction of the intelligent skepticism with which the new journalists were greeted. That skepticism is still with us—we occasionally read about dark suspicions that television newscasters are selected for their healthy hair or sparkling teeth. All these suspicions anticipate the difficulties introduced by television into broadcast journalism.

With the introduction of television, pictures began to play a more important role in news reporting than they had ever held in print journalism. Films from remote locations, edited to emphasize the dramatic highlights, gave viewers more information than words ever did, but there was no method for evaluating the impact or meaning of the pictures. The importance of pictures has been vastly underrated by most critics, including many newscasters themselves. In late 1974 one broadcaster of a network news program argued that "television cannot provide all the news a person needs to be informed. A half-hour newscast contains less words than the front page of the *New York Times*." He neglected to add that it also contains pictures that convey emotions and a variety of data that never find their way onto the front page of a newspaper—or the inside pages, for that matter.

Television news is often treated by critics as if it were words accompanied by pictures of little importance. There is no reliable information available about how film or video tape reports influence viewers' understanding of events, and this unknown factor in television news is a source of frustration to critics. Some critics, assuming that pictures have great impact, have argued that the peace movement of the 1960s was stimulated by reactions to the televised coverage of war in a primitive land and that the black revolution was stimulated by the portrayal of affluence on television—a way of life that did not fit with the private experience of many blacks. Television, as they see it, is a revolutionary force that is not in the control of any group. Other critics have argued that television news is superficial, glib, oriented toward show-business values, and the victim of concern about audience ratings. It should be, they argue, more like a newspaper. In short, the evaluation of television news is a lively field for the critic because radically different evaluations are widely accepted.

The Issues

A number of the current issues with which critics are concerned are discussed below.

The lack of investigative reporting. Television reporters are often considered, by print journalists, to be the people who arrive at a press conference at the last minute, film the public announcement, and leave immediately for another prepackaged public announcement. Television newscasters are, according to this stereotype, not the people who are likely to do background preparation for a report. They substitute interviews for the less spectacular work to be accomplished by digging in public records, searching in archives, or sifting through the records of many other interviews.

There are reasons for this lack of investigative reporting. First, the results of background research are frequently more suitable for print than visual presentation. In addition, television film crews are expensive and are usually sent out on assignment only when there is a good possibility of producing a story that can be used on the air. The result is that background investigation is frequently neglected.

There are other pressures which operate to the disadvantage of the investigative reporter. Television news producers are often concerned with the sizes of their audiences. There is great fear that a thorough background treatment on any subject except the most current and controversial might result in a loss of audience. The consequence, once again, is a disinclination to conduct investigations which do not relate to immediate "headline" stories.

Finally, television news lacks the tradition and enjoyment of the investigative "scoop" that newspaper journalists enjoy. The *Washington Post* and *New York Times* enjoyed considerable notoriety for their roles in the publication of the Pentagon Papers provided by Daniel Ellsberg and for their work on the Watergate investigation. Robert Woodward, Carl Bernstein, and the other reporters who dug out the Watergate story were said to be working "in the best traditions of investigative journalism." There is no such tradition in broadcasting, however, and the reward for such activity may be a complaint to the FCC.

This last point may be worth further consideration. Radio and television stations, licensed by the federal government in "the public interest, convenience and necessity," are vulnerable to pressure groups. If an investigative report caused a complaint to be filed with the FCC, the management of the station might find its license in jeopardy. A prudent manager naturally wishes to avoid that risk and consequently may be unwilling to take any risks, including those involved in investigative reporting.

The audience may also play a role in the lack of investigative reporting. Although we praise newspapers for taking chances and exposing offenses against the public, we often talk of television and radio as destructive forces to be contained. We sometimes suspect that they cause violence, lend themselves to demagoguery, and are superficial. If the Watergate story had been pursued by an NBC or CBS newsperson, would we honor the network? Or would we decry the abuse of the power the networks enjoy and accuse them of violating a public trust?

The preference for the visual. One of the unproven but widely accepted assumptions about television news producers is that, given a choice, most of them select trivial stories accompanied by interesting visual material in preference to "important" but non-visual stories. This can result in two problems: the omission of significant events and the distortion of those that are reported.

The ways in which omission occurs can be easily checked. For example, the stories reported on television can be compared with those reported in a newspaper. It is best done for a given community using local television news and a local newspaper. There may be gross omissions, or, as some Boston students discovered last year, television may have covered the major stories but omitted *side-bar* stories, the secondary items that fill out viewers' understanding of events. In any case, the omission question can be dealt with quantitatively.

The problem of distortion is subtler and more difficult to explore. Television news emphasizes the dramatic moment in events. For example, Senator Edward Muskie wept when, in the midst of a tense campaign, he learned that a New Hampshire newspaper publisher had criticized his wife. It was a minor event, unrelated to the issues at stake in the campaign, but it was widely reported because of its human interest. Did this clarify the campaign issues for the voter, or was it an example of television selecting the dramatic at the expense of the important?

Another example occurred during the 1968 Democratic National Convention in Chicago, when television cameras reported the conflict between demonstrators and the Chicago police, which resulted in a "police riot." Critics suggested that the television newscasters should have stayed with the issues inside the hall rather than featuring the demonstrators. As events developed, the riot was the major issue of the day—of the year—and the "issues" in the hall were of lesser importance. Would events have been different, however, if the networks had not reported the demonstrations in detail?

Yet another example involves President John F. Kennedy, who was often reported during his televised news conferences as exchanging witty banter with reporters. Evening news roundups ocassionally neglected more substantial portions of the conferences in favor of these lighter moments. President Richard M. Nixon was angered because the moments from his press conferences in which he had heated exchanges with CBS reporter Dan Rather were often selected for repetition in evening broadcasts. Were television producers serving their audiences well or badly in making these news judgments in favor of the visual, the interesting, and the human as opposed to the abstract, the subtle, and perhaps the more enduring issues?

There is no categorical answer that can describe the visual tendency of television news. One cannot say, with any accuracy, that television consistently prefers visual trivia to other news. Yet, there is a decision to be made on each news item. The extent to which it is visually interesting is one factor that is considered. It is the job of the critic, not to make bold and superficial generalizations, but to ask of individual news stories, Was it worth reporting? Was it apparently used more for its visual than for its news value? Was the moment excerpted from an interview of significance or merely of interest? Was the viewer persuaded that she or he has been exposed to the most meaningful events, and parts of events, or merely those that were easy to report, easy to visualize, and easy to watch?

The shortage of time. There are times at many newspapers when there is more space available than there is news to fill it—on a Thursday, for instance, when retail advertising is heavy and the "news hole" is enlarged, or on a preholiday Sunday, when added advertising creates a need for more news. This is the time when background reports, essays, and features find their way into our living rooms—a luxury almost unknown in television.

Television operates within severe, almost crippling, time restraints. The half-hour news program may have from twenty-one to twenty-three minutes of news, including weather and sports. Only the most unusual events are accorded more than three minutes of air time, or 350 words of news copy. If a minor event is given thirty seconds, the news reporter can devote fewer than 100 words to the event. Half an hour is simply not enough time for a thorough report on the events of the day.

This press of time means that only the most salient features of an event can be reported. It means that a shorthand must be used in which public figures are encouraged to summarize their views on difficult policies in a few seconds. Actors on the public stage are assigned to "teams." Teams are given "positions" to defend. Conflict is reported as existing between individuals rather than between philosophic or political viewpoints. The spokesperson is treated as if he or she were the position. Public affairs comes to resemble sports. No problem is too vast or too subtle to be summarized between commercial announcements. The world consists of short bursts of unrelated information.

Difficult as it may be, time is somewhat less of a problem now than it was twelve years ago, when fifteen-minute local news reports were common. In many markets, beginning the the autumn of 1975, the evening news block was extended to ninety minutes. In addition, the networks have used such programs as "Sixty Minutes" to dig in greater depth into specific stories, and the level of journalistic judgment demonstrated on such programs is frequently admirable.

The need for verification. More than one network reporter has sent a "scoop" back to headquarters only to find out that the news producers held the story until it was "verified" by a wire service. At times, this prudence has saved potential embarrassment. Prudence, however, is different from timidity, and some critics have suspected that it is courage that is missing from television news.

Again, there is little to be gained from general discussions of larger issues, such as Watergate and the networks. The issue is already available for examination in local communities. Most controversial stories, such as those concerning malfeasance in public office or corporations that are in difficulty, will usually be carried first by the local newspaper.

All of the characteristics of television news mentioned above work against the reporter with a controversial story. Time is not available, funds are usually not available to support investigative reporting, stories which have not been pre-reported in another medium are usually not visual, and the "easy" judgment for a producer is against using such stories. Thus, television and radio news producers work in an environment in which prudence is rewarded and journalistic enterprise is risky and undersupported. One of the contributions critics can make to broadcast journalism is to call attention to the extent to which radio and television break stories or wait for verification before following other media.

Television favors pre-reported news. When television news producers decide to cover an event, they commit several people and hundreds of dollars—perhaps thousands—to that story. Since they have limited resources, their decision to cover one event necessarily means that other stories will not be covered. It is important that the crew bring a story back from an assignment. It is helpful if they can pick up two or more stories while they are out, so those events that are tightly scheduled and convenient to reach are favored. This means that stories that are planned —or pre-reported—and that are of known news value are most likely to be covered.

Although larger stations keep one camera crew and reporter free for late-breaking stories, such as accidents, news programs are built around such pre-arranged events as press conferences by public officials, scheduled protest demonstrations by well-known groups, sports events, strikes that are planned, conferences by public and educational groups, interviews set up in advance, and recurring events, such as lighting of municipal Christmas trees, Fourth of July parades, opening of amusement parks, first day of school, and commencements. It is possible for a news producer to plan the usage of the film crew well in advance when events such as these are covered.

Spontaneous events are difficult to cover, because it is not known how long they will occupy a camera crew, where they will occur, or whether they will produce a story appropriate for use on the air. Although news is, by definition, concerned with spontaneous events, it is much simpler, more economical of time and money, and is more dependable to include pre-arranged events in newscasts.

Newsmakers, those who are the objects of the public's concern, are aware that they are most likely to be covered on the air if they include radio and television news reporters in their plans. As a consequence, much news is scheduled to occur at times and places convenient for reporters and film crews. This is, of course, true of newspaper journalism as well as broadcasting, but the clumsiness of the arrangements have made it increasingly common for newsmakers to plan "news" with television coverage in mind. At times, television "consultants"—often reporters— provide advice on how news should occur if television coverage is to be maximized.

Although all of the procedures described above seem commonplace, the result has been a drastic alteration in the relation of the news reporting mechanism to "reality." Traditionally, reporters and publishers have been thought to be observers of events. We assume that they do not influence the events they report. Television is so dominant a medium, so expensive, that this traditional observer role has been changed. Television coverage frequently becomes the focus of the event, and the result is a tail-wagging-the-dog phenomenon in which events are subservient to the coverage they receive in the broadcast media.

In 1962 historian Daniel J. Boorstin published *The Image or What Happened to the American Dream*, a "how-not-to-do-it" book about "our arts of self-deception."[1] In it, Boorstin angrily argued that our public media are preoccupied with "pseudo-events," which (1) are "planned, planted or incited," (2) are planned for the purpose of being reported, (3) have an ambiguous "relation to the underlying reality," and (4) are usually self-fulfilling prophecies.

If one accepts Marshall McLuhan's notion that the media function in society somewhat analogously to the function of the central nervous system in the body, all of this seems rather labored and unnecessary. The media seem to distort "reality" only because those of us who are older were accustomed to an older version of reality. From this point of view, the transformation of news from sporadic coverage of chance events to the systematic coverage of planned events is merely one predictable characteristic of our post-industrial electronic society. Besides, one may ask, who is to say that planned events are less interesting, less important or less worthy of coverage than an unplanned explosion or accident?

Boorstin argues that pseudo-events are acceptable only because they appear in the guise of spontaneous events. One suspects that the audience would be less interested in news if the newscaster began his or her report, "Here are some events which we have connived to bring about today." Spontaneous news is diluted by pseudo-events, Boorstin argues, and viewers are misled when they are encouraged to accept press conferences and contrived demonstrations as news.

For the critic, the distinction between non-media reality and pseudo-events deserves investigation. A news program consisting of interviews, conferences, parades, and other pre-arranged events is different from one in which such events are minimized. No matter which side of the argument we find persuasive, we can only increase our understanding of broadcasting if we ask the question, "Would this have occurred at all, or occurred differently, if radio and television were not available to report it?"

Current Issues

Issues in broadcast news occur frequently, usually have a short life, and are often reported as being basic to the well-being of the republic. Perhaps we are unusually aware of them because broadcast journalists respond to them with unusual intensity. Following is a short list of recent and current issues which is suggestive of the kinds of issues that may occur in the future.

1. It has been charged that television and radio news, as the activity of corporations with vested interests in defense and other economic activities, is influenced by what is thought to be the corporate well-being. Anti-war activists were particularly enamored of this argument. Harry Skornia, author of *Television and the News*, is perhaps the most eloquent advocate of this point of view.

2. It has been charged that network news is heavily biased by reporters, producers, and writers, all of whom share an Eastern liberal view of public life. Edith Efron is the best-known advocate of this point of view, and her charges, which appeared in *The News Twisters*, created something of a stir in the early 1970s, appearing shortly after similar charges by then Vice President Spiro Agnew. Two other studies, based on her charges, arrived at contradictory judgments.

3. There is concern about the spread of what has been dubbed "tabloid" broadcast journalism in some markets. Characterized by a fast pace, short items, extensive use of film, and an emphasis on accidents and other unplanned events, tabloid news is seen by some as the bad money that may drive the good money out of the market.

4. Film continues to be considered desirable by audiences—as judged by ratings—but of dubious journalistic value. The criticism that television news emphasizes the visual at the expense of the substantial remains a point of concern.

5. New video tape equipment, which is simpler and more portable and which eliminates the processing delay inherent in the use of film, is available and is beginning to be used in some markets. It is expected that this technological change will increase both the out-of-studio content in news programs and the flexibility of broadcasters.

6. The time devoted to television news in many markets is increasing. As more time is devoted to news, an interesting problem to be considered by critics is how the additional time should be used.

7. There is considerable concern that news, both in print and on the air, can be "managed" by skillful public officials. Among the techniques used are the timing of news releases for maximum coverage, giving exclusive information to "friendly" reporters, limiting access to the information upon which news reports are based, arranging "leaks" so that unauthorized and unattributed stories will appear, background briefings in which public officials press their point of view but do not permit the source to be identified, the timing of news releases containing unfavorable information so that minimum coverage will result, and the release of misleading information by public officials.

    There is, of course, nothing new in this catalogue of attempts to influence public opinion. The attempted cover-up of the White House involvement in the Watergate burglary has focused public attention on the prevalence of these techniques. For critics, the detection and exposure of news management is a constant challenge.

8. The development of "all-news" radio formats presents interesting opportunities for broadcast journalists. Typically, a story is "followed" with up-dates at regular intervals. There is some likelihood that independent television stations may experiment with an "all-news" television format in the near future. Such formats present the opportunity for the back-grounding, the depth, and the analysis broadcast news has lacked in the past. The task for critics is to determine whether this opportunity is being taken or whether "all-news" is merely a repetition of the kind of news which formerly existed in the shorter news program.

9. News consultants are being used by many stations in an effort to improve their audience ratings. Typically, consultants use surveys, content analysis, and other research techniques to make a series of recommendations to management. Management consulting is, of course, a routine activity in many industries. Critics are concerned, however, that news consultants base their recommendations upon "show business" or audience values rather than upon journalistic values. A useful discussion can be found in *Moments of Truth*, edited by Marvin Barrett.

In this chapter we have attempted to focus on the underlying issues in broadcast journalism and to direct the reader to some of the current issues. It is unlikely that the issues identified here will be "current" for very long. The task for critics is to identify the underlying issues which link the specific issues which may occur from time to time.

Note

1. Daniel J. Boorstin, *The Image or What Happened to the American Dream* (New York: Atheneum Publishers, 1962), p. iii.

Suggested Readings

Adams, William, and Fay Schreibman, eds. *Television Network News: Issues in Content Research*. Washington: George Washington University, 1979. An examination of research methods and application of them to network news.

Bagdikian, Ben H. *The Information Machines*. New York: Harper and Row, 1971. The best single source for information about television news and its relation to print.

Barrett, Marvin, ed. *Moments of Truth: The Fifth Alfred I. Dupont-Columbia University Survey of Broadcast Journalism*. New York: Thomas Y. Crowell, 1975. Useful information about television and Watergate, the use of news consultants, etc.

Boorstin, Daniel J. *The Image or What Happened to the American Dream*. New York: Atheneum Publishers, 1962.

Diamond, Edwin. *The Tin Kazoo: Television, Politics and the News*. Cambridge: MIT Press, 1975. A readable exploration of the relations among the three entities in its title.

Efron, Edith. *The News Twisters*. Los Angeles, California: Nash Publications, 1971. A methodologically unsound analysis of news which points to a liberal bias in network news reports. Much discussed at time of publication.

Epstein, Edward Jay. *News from Nowhere: Television and the News.* New York: Random House, 1973. Interesting inside information on NBC news in a balanced presentation.

Friendly, Fred W. *Due to Circumstances Beyond Our Control.* New York: Random House, 1967. The former president of CBS news explains how decisions are made at the network level.

Gans, Herbert J. *Deciding What's News: A Study of the CBS Evening News, NBC Nightly News, Newsweek and Time.* New York: Pantheon Books, 1979. The most complex and subtle treatment of the questions raised by a number of critics.

Keeley, Joseph. *The Left Leaning Antenna: Political Bias in Television.* New Rochelle, New York: Arlington House, 1971. Similar to Efron's study but without providing access to the sources used.

Kendrick, Alexander. *Prime Time: The Life of Edward R. Murrow.* Boston: Little, Brown and Company, 1969. The way it was.

LeRoy, David J., and Christopher H. Sterling, eds. *Mass News: Practices, Controversies and Alternatives.* Englewood Cliffs, New Jersey: Prentice-Hall, 1973. Good source of material for discussions of news.

Mayer, Martin. *About Television.* New York: Harper and Row, 1972. The chapter devoted to news points to the shortcomings of the present system. Although less critical in tone, it is far more damning than Friendly's assessment.

Mertz, Robert. *CBS: Reflections in a Bloodshot Eye.* Chicago: Playboy Press, 1975.

Powers, Ron. *The Newscasters: The News Business as Show Business.* New York: St. Martin's Press, 1977. An examination of the importance of entertainment values and their influence on both local and network news programs.

Rubin, Barry. *International News and the American Media.* Beverly Hills: Sage Publications, 1977. An examination of news from abroad in the American media, and the role of profit in determining what is covered.

Small, William. *To Kill a Messenger: Television News and the Real World.* New York: Hastings House, 1970. A knowledgeable assessment of television and Vietnam.

Skornia, Harry J. *Television and the News.* Palo Alto, California: Pacific Books, 1968. The author points to the corporate structure of network news as a serious shortcoming. An angry, exciting book.

Stevenson, Robert L., et al. "Untwisting *The News Twisters*: A Replication of Efron's Study," *Journalism Quarterly* 50 (Summer 1973). A repetition of Efron's study leading to radically different conclusions. Efron responded in the Spring 1974 JQ.

Tuchman, Gaye. *Making News: A Study of the Construction of Reality.* New York: Free Press, 1978. An examination of journalism, both print and electronic, in the context of a broad concern about the effects of editorial decisions.

Weaver, Paul H. "Is Television News Biased?" *The Public Interest* 49 (Winter 1972). The most persuasive case against the networks, based upon a sophisticated analysis of the industry.

Cable Television and the New Media

For more than a decade critics have talked about the "electronic revolution" that was about to occur. Some changes occurred, most notably the development of cable television systems, but the revolution seemed slow in coming. Home Box Office, Inc., began to offer pay television services. In Columbus, Ohio, Warner Cable experimented with the QUBE system: a two-way interactive system that allowed viewers to respond to instructions, questions, or to express program choices. The system has been used to test products, to provide an almost instant measure of public opinion, and to test educational programming. In Atlanta, Ted Turner, America's Cup skipper and owner of a UHF station, made arrangements to have his programs carried on a number of cable systems across the country. The result was a "super station": a station seen in dozens of towns and cities without using landlines. Satellites enabled the Public Broadcasting System to create a network without the heavy expense of renting land facilities from AT&T. In India, a satellite was used to distribute agricultural and health information. Although very little appeared to change on screens as we watched the CBS Evening News, the revolution had, in fact, occurred. What most of us were watching was the last of the old system. And the new system? Who could guess what it might be? Comsat, Inc., hopes to have direct satellite-to-home systems in operation by 1983. If they are successful, both conventional broadcasting *and* cable may find themselves obsolescent!

The Birth of Cable

In the 1950s the number of television stations increased dramatically. Audiences in some parts of the country, however, suffered from terrain which made it difficult for them to receive the signals. Not only were mountains often obstacles to signals, but no single private individual was likely to have or expend the resources to import a signal for his or her home from a mountaintop location. If several families were willing to pay for the service,

77

however, it might be practicable and even profitable. This solution was applied in a number of states beginning in 1948 and resulted in the growth of a number of small "community antenna" systems in Pennsylvania, California, Vermont, Oregon, and Montana.

In the late fifties it was noted that cable television, as it became called, had advantages for urban dwellers: the cable system could import otherwise unavailable signals from distant cities; it could provide channels for local programming; and it offered the potential for pay-television channels. Some promoters talked of adding burglar alarm services or access to centralized computers for shopping or library research as an eventual part of the cable service. Others talked about the possibility of having access, through cable, to a central storage system from which prorgrams could be selected and played at will. Cable television seemed to be the medium for a rapid advance in communication services to the public.

From Entrepreneur to Corporation

Most of the first generation, pre-1965 cable operators were entrepreneurs in the classical tradition of American business. They saw a market for a service and offered it as quickly and cheaply as possible. Many of them sold their service door-to-door, bargaining with telephone and electric companies for space on poles, setting rates according to what the market would bear, and managing to stay in business. Cable systems seemed to operate at the same level of management sophistication as, say, an independent auto repair shop.

In the mid-1960s a number of corporations identified the potential growth and the protected market for cable systems and began to enter the field. Some broadcasters, such as CBS, entered the field to protect the distribution of their signals but were later forced out by federal regulations. Of the new corporations, the most aggressive and best known was Teleprompter. It purchased local stations at a substantial profit for the founding owner and applied for franchises when no system existed in a desirable market. New names began to appear in the communications industry: Viacom, Warner Cable, Cox Cable, Cypress Communications, National Transvideo, and a host of others.

This period of growth was not without difficulties. Cable systems were expensive to install, particularly with the higher technical standards which became effective in 1966. Broadcasters,

concerned about the survival of on-air broadcasting, lobbied successfully for legislation which would protect the existing industry.
And money, in enormous quantities, was needed to finance the
new industry—one estimate in 1970 was that two billion dollars
would be needed by 1975 to finance expansion. With the 1971
increase in interest rates, cable corporations experienced severe difficulties in maintaining their level of growth. The result was a
shrinkage in stock values, a failure to provide many of the services
promised in the earlier days, and a postponement of the planned
growth of the industry. The cable television story is a remarkable
one—from boom to recession in less than ten years!

If cable television is speculative and expensive to enter, one
may ask why it is so attractive to business interests. The answer
is partly that it is a semi-monopoly—once cable operators have
a franchise, their investment is protected. Another answer is that
the potential profits are enormous. If an urban cable system
achieves a 50 percent penetration (one out of every two families
subscribe), profits are estimated to be in excess of 25 percent of
gross income. Estimates vary, of course, and each system is different. However, the potential for a sizable profit is present. Further, some investors are able to take advantage, for tax purposes,
of the initial losses reported by almost all systems.

Cable is speculative, potentially profitable, and has made and
lost large sums of money for operators and investors. It is an
exciting new system for distributing communication signals. For
all these reasons, it attracts the entrepreneur, the communications
visionary, and the reformer. All find in it possibilities for achiev-
ing their particular goals.

Cable and Government

Open-circuit, whether AM, FM, or television, is regulated by
the FCC because of the limited number of channels. The argument
for regulation is based upon the assumption that a scarce public
resource—the spectrum—should be used "in the public interest,
convenience and necessity." Cable distribution systems with many
channels may appear, superficially, to need less regulation, perhaps
even none at all. That has not been the case. There are several
reasons for regulating cable television, none of them simple.

First, although it is possible for a town or city to have more
than one cable system, it makes little sense to divide the market
and increase installation costs. It would be rather like having

two water companies in the same town. As a consequence, cable television franchises issued by town or city governments are normally considered monopolies. Towns therefore bargain hard to get the maximum advantage from their franchises, engaging legal counsel, holding hearings, and otherwise proceeding in a regulatory manner.

Second, a number of abuses in the 1960s—the bribing of local officials, for instance—led to a concern about cable television on the part of some state governments. The result was a variety of regulatory agencies or commissions at the state level, which, to varying degrees, attempt to secure a uniformity of able service from one town to another, regulate rates, and set technical standards.

A third tier of regulation exists at the federal level. The FCC, concerned about the siphoning of programs from on-air broadcasters without compensation, issued a number of regulations concerning technical standards, the number of signals which may be imported by cable operators from outside their home markets, and rules concerning other similar matters.

From the viewpoint of the cable operators, the three-tier system of regulation is restrictive, complicated, overlapping, and at times inconsistent. From their standpoint, one level of regulation is sufficient. They argue that local communities can determine their needs, that the FCC should allow the marketplace to decide the future of on-air broadcasting, and that state regulation is unnecessary. Although there is no clear viewpoint to which all cable operators would agree, most seem to favor local regulation and dislike state regulation.

There are good economic reasons for the operators to favor local regulation. Since most of them operate in several markets, they have access to information and to economies which may not come to the attention of inexpert local officials or citizen groups. On the whole, state agencies have restrained cable systems from neglecting local communities, and federal regulation has operated to insure that cable systems do not upset the existing system. One does not have to look far to determine why cable operators oppose three-tier regulation.

Formal federal involvement with the regulation of cable television began in 1962, when the FCC asserted its interest in a microwave system serving a cable company. In 1965 the FCC asserted authority over all systems served by microwave but did not attempt to regulate those which did not depend upon microwave service.[1] The First Report and Order, as it is known, argued that on-air service, particularly by UHF stations, needed protection from cable competition. Eleven months later the FCC issued the Second Report and Order, reaffirming its jurisdiction over all cable systems, and established a policy for the importation of signals from distant stations.[2]

In 1968 the FCC encouraged local cable operators to originate programs. In October 1969 it ruled that systems with more than 3,500 subscribers were responsible for originating local programs. In 1972 the FCC issued new regulations which added urgency to the requirement for local origination and established four classes of channels which could provide a variety of services: retransmission of off-air signals, distribution of system-originated programs, carrying of signals from receivers for pay television, and subscriber-originated signals.

The local-origination rule was neither popular nor successful, and in November 1974 the FCC scrapped it, conceding that the original rule had resulted in large expenditures and little benefit. It adopted, instead, a rule requiring cable firms with more than 3,500 subscribers to have equipment available for the production and origination of programs by local groups. The FCC thus ruled that access was the issue rather than the need for a continuing local program service.

The most interesting of the FCC's regulations have been those associated with retransmission.[3] Pulled between a desire to encourage cable and a stronger desire to maintain the existing system, the FCC has limited the number of signals a cable system may import (those more than 35 miles away or meeting a signal-strength test). The limitations are: (1) in the top fifty television markets, three networks may be carried if not provided locally and three non-affiliated (independent) stations; (2) in the next fifty markets, the cable system is limited to providing the three network signals (if they are not available from local stations) and two non-affiliated stations; and (3) smaller markets receive somewhat more protection from imported signals. In addition, the FCC required that all local public television stations be carried, as well as those having a Grade B (relatively strong) signal in the area. Other public stations may be carried in the absence of objections from local public stations.

One curious result of the FCC's rules is that for major markets, which are already well-served, the number of signals imported will increase, whereas small markets will receive a smaller number of imported signals. This decision was evidently made to provide financial protection for smaller market stations, which often operate with slender profit margins.

In addition, the FCC requires that cable systems in the top

one hundred markets have a twenty-channel capability. Cable operators have argued that it would be sufficient if systems provided all required services "plus one" channel which could be activated when required.

At the moment many systems do not have a twenty-channel capability and otherwise fall short of the FCC's technical requirements.

Pay Television

Although pay television systems have operated using on-the-air signals on an experimental basis, most people concerned with pay television think of cable as the most desirable distribution system for their programs. In 1968 the FCC issued rules regulating the content of pay television (then called subscription television) systems. In 1970 it applied the rules to pay cable systems and in 1972 included the rules in their Third Report and Order. At that time the rules restricted access to feature films between two and ten years old and sports events that had been broadcast in the past two years, and they limited the percentage of total pay cable offerings that could be devoted to movies and sports.

Despite these limitations, pay television continued to attract the attention of entrepreneurs. There were a number of reasons for this interest. First, pay television would have consumers pay directly for the product, as they do when purchasing a book or a ticket to a play or concert. The result could be a more immediate reward for producers of successful shows than is possible in the on-air systems in which successful shows are rewarded with future contracts rather than immediate earnings.

A second reason for interest in cable is that the viewers might select only programs attractive to them. The lower-level-of-viewing-attention which presumably accounts for a substantial part of the commercial television audience would be missing. This *might* result in an increase in quality.

Third, programs of minority interest (both ethnic and cultural) might be provided, *if* the audience were willing to pay the higher cost-per-viewer necessary to make it attractive to the cable programmer.

In these ways, pay television offers possible solutions to some of the nagging problems of the present system. However, it does involve some trade-offs: the impulse viewing which provides such a large prime-time audience might be decreased; the program sources which have been developed for commercial television might not survive in a pay television market; and, if the commercial system were unable to sustain the quality of its programs, including news, lower income families might have access to needed information or entertainment only at a sacrifice.

In March 1975 the FCC announced new regulations for pay cable television: (1) Pay television operators may bid on films less than three years old or more than ten years old even if the pictures are under a non-exclusive contract to networks or stations. (2) Pay television firms are required to maintain a public file in which titles, dates of showing, and the section of the rules permitting the showing are listed. Also, any details of contracts to networks or stations must be included. (3) The pay television market size will be determined by the best signal coverage area of local conventional stations carried on the system. (4) Although pay television cannot carry specific events carried by broadcasters within the preceding five years, such as bowl games, access to these events under a formula was allowed.

Although these rules were liberalized somewhat from the earlier ones, several cable firms announced plans to appeal the rules in the courts. At the same time, cable companies made plans to offer new program services on a pay basis beginning in the summer of 1975. Further, Home Box Office, a subsidiary of Time, Inc., began a pay television network linked by cable systems in the fall of 1975. Cable operators have depended on promise rather than performance in selling their services. Hampered by FCC restrictions and, in some states, by difficulties in raising their rates, they nevertheless remain optimistic about the long-term prospects of cable.

Cable and Critics

Cable is an exciting financial opportunity for entrepreneurs and offers potential benefits to the public in additional services. But what is the role of critics in all of this? Should they remain passive, reacting to programs delivered on cable in the same way as those delivered on air? Or are there special considerations which critics should give to the problems and potential of cable? The latter is certainly the case—there are a number of concerns to which critics should give their attention.

1. Critics can make certain that the public is aware of the contents and implications of franchise agreements made between

the town or city and the cable operator. Critics may compare them to other agreements or seek comment on them by those with experience in the field.

2. Critics can call attention to the public access channel provided on the cable and provide critical response to the programs. Here, since the performers are not professionals, an interesting question of criteria emerges. The critics may perhaps find it useful to evaluate such programs in terms of their stated goals, rather than compare them to the programs on public and commercial stations. Critics may raise such questions as: Who is using the public access channel? Is the content of general interest or is it specialized? What community problems or needs are not dealt with in public access programming? Who pays for the cost of public access programming? Are there unused program resources in the community?

3. The FCC required that each system reserve one channel for the use of educational institutions. Critics might consider: Is the channel used? Are the offerings promoted? Who is responsible for program decisions? To what extent are the educational needs of the community being met through this channel?

4. Each cable operator is required to maintain a local government access channel. Concerning it, critics might ask: Do governmental agencies or officials use the channel to their own advantage? Does the local government make the best possible use of the channel? What governmental problems might be solved or alleviated using the channel?

5. Are the non-program possibilities of the cable system explored and utilized, or is the potential neglected? At the moment, for financial reasons, neglect is the common practice, but the critic will have a constructive role to play at some happier time in the future.

In summary, cable television is a system rather than a program and may seem resistant to critical evaluation. However, critics have a vital role to play in protecting the public interest by insisting upon adequate performance by cable operators. New program forms will call for new styles and criteria for evaluation. Critics can find their own horizons extended by the challenge of evaluating "non-professional" programs. Finally, critics can be an important information link between the audience and the cable operator. New services will not be utilized unless an audience is aware of them and knows how to use them. These issues should provide sufficient difficulty to keep any critic busy for the foreseeable future.

And the New Media

Cable television distribution systems are but the first of the technological changes occuring about us. By themselves, cable television systems merely deliver local signals with improved image quality and two or three out of town channels ("imported"), plus a local and, perhaps, educational channel. When combined with satellite delivery systems, however, cable systems can provide local distribution of signals from distant places.

The possibilities became obvious in mid-1979 when the FCC lifted a three-year moratorium on the carriage of video signals on AT&T's Comstar satellite. This gave the U.S. three satellite systems for domestic use: Western Union has three "birds" in its Westar system; RCA has two in its Satcom system; and AT&T and GTE, in cooperation, have Comstar.

The results of these many program channels can be quickly summarized: in 1979 more than 10,000 movies, 2,500 sports events, 7,000 hours of children's programs, two 24-hour news services and the Spanish International network.

In mid-1980, WTCG—the first "super station"—will begin its own satellite-and-cable news service. Both public television and public radio are using satellite facilities.

The revolution has not been limited to commercial operators and government agencies. Home video recording systems now cost little more than a black-and-white television set in the 1950s, and in some homes the video collection will soon rival the record collection.

The problems associated with these developments are multiple. In this country, networks anticipate the fragmentation of the audiences for their entertainment programs. Abroad, there is a concern among developing nations that the industrial powers may monopolize the available frequencies and the space available for satellites, leaving them in a perpetual communication dependence. Tanzania, in 1979, took the unusual step of deciding not to develop its own television system because it would benefit only the privileged few, not the masses. Most less developed countries (LDCs) opted for participation, however, and have pressed for frequency and space reservations so that they will have a place in which to develop their communication systems in the future.

And what is the role of the critic in response to these changes? Perhaps the most useful approach is to regard technological change as a problem in public policy, an opportunity to defend the public interest.

A few of the systems competing for the public's time and discretionary income are: cable television; pay-cable; subscription TV (pay programs sent over-the-air); and informational systems (up to 200 pages of data on file for use on command by viewers). Others are on the way. There is an important journalistic role to be played in informing the public about them, and a critical role to be played in the evaluation of the competing systems.

Notes

1. 30 FCC, 683 (1965).
2. 2 FCC, 2d725 (1966).
3. 36 FCC, 2d141 (1972).

Suggested Readings

Adler, Richard, and Walter S. Baer. *Aspen Notebook: Cable and Continuing Education*. New York: Praeger, 1973. Contains a useful bibliography that ranges beyond the topic of the book.

Adler, Richard, and Walter S. Baer. *The Electronic Box Office: Humanities and Arts on the Cable*. New York: Praeger, 1974. A useful discussion of pay television, how it works, and how it relates to minority program preferences.

Baer, Walter S. *Cable Television: A Handbook for Decision-Making*. New York: Crane-Russak, 1973. Prepared by the National Science Foundation as a citizen guide.

LeDuc, Donald R. *Cable Television*. A Selected Annotated Bibliography. Falls Church, Virginia: ERIC Clearinghouse on Reading and Communication Skills, Speech Module, SCA, 1975.

LeDuc, Donald R. *Cable Television and the FCC: A Crisis in Media Control*. Philadelphia: Temple University Press, 1973. A thorough and accurate account of the FCC's cable policies. It appeared after the major changes and is not seriously dated.

Martin, James. *The Wired Society*. Englewood Cliffs: Prentice-Hall, 1978. An excellent source of information about the new technologies and their possible effects on the telecommunication industries and on society.

Newman, Joseph, ed. *Wiring the World: The Explosion in Communications*. Washington, D.C.: Books by U.S. News and World Report, 1971. A period piece that shows some of the thinking of the euphoric period of cable expansion. It may be timely again, but, even if not, it serves as a good statement of what might be achieved.

Phillips, Mary Alice Mayer. *CATV: A History of Community Antenna Television.* Evanston, Illinois: Northwestern University Press, 1972.

Pool, Ithiel de Sola. *Talking Back: Citizen Feedback and Cable Technology.* Cambridge, Massachusetts: MIT Press, 1973. Contains an interesting article by Martin Mayer on "Cable and the Arts" and some information of a technical nature not readily available.

Rivkin, Steven R. *A New Guide to Federal Cable Television Regulations.* Cambridge: MIT Press, 1978. A valuable collection of regulatory documents together with a summary of the current status of research in cable.

Robinson, Glen O., ed. *Communications for Tomorrow: Policy Perspectives for the 1980's.* New York: Praeger Special Studies, 1978. One of the few books on regulatory matters written with a knowledgeable eye on future possibilities.

Sloan Commission on Cable Television. *On the Cable: The Television of Abundance.* New York: McGraw-Hill, 1971. A good summary of the potential of cable as seen in the late 1960s.

Smith, Ralph Lee. *The Wired Nation: The Electronic Communications Highway.* New York: Harper and Row, 1972. A good survey from the viewpoint of community interest, with a good bibliography.

Sterling, Christopher H. *Mass Communications and Society.* A Selected Annotated Bibliography. Falls Church, Virginia: ERIC Clearinghouse on Reading and Communication Skills, Speech Module, SCA, 1975.

Social Effects and the Criticism of Broadcasting

We noted earlier that critics often turn away from television or radio programming and evaluate other aspects of the medium: problems of control, program strategy, governmental regulation, or access to the media. One of the concerns of those who do not restrict themselves to the evaluation of programs involves the effects that radio and television have on society.

This concern is not new. In the 1930s many people became alarmed over the possibilities of political control when radio was used by demagogues or those with skill in broadcasting. The names associated with early political broadcasting read like a roll call of controversial figures of the period: Dr. John Brinkley, who ran for the governorship of Kansas after having his license to practice medicine revoked; Huey Long, who ran for the governorship of Louisiana on one of the earliest "media" campaigns; Father Coughlin, who changed his support from Franklin Roosevelt to Long and, for a time, appeared to be a potent political force; Roosevelt himself, whose "fireside chats" could not be matched for political effectiveness by any other political figure of his time; and Adolf Hitler, one of the first totalitarians to use broadcasting for domestic political control and as a weapon in foreign aggression.

The concern about the effects of such broadcasting led to a great deal of research, much of it reported by Paul Lazarsfeld, a pioneer in mass communication research, and his colleagues at Columbia University. There were, of course, other reactions, notably the formation of the Institute for Propaganda Analysis, which operated on the assumption that clear thinking—the ability to spot logical fallacies in broadcasts—was a defense against propaganda.

If any single event dramatized the potential effects of radio, it was the adaptation of H. G. Wells's *War of the Worlds* broadcast by Orson Welles on his Mercury Theatre on Halloween night, 1938. Fortunately, Hadley Cantril, a sociologist, was preparing an investigation of radio and was able to gather information about the effects of the broadcast. He reported that "at least a million Americans became frightened and thousands were panic stricken."[1] Both Cantril's report and recordings of the original broadcast are available for those interested in comparing the stimulus with a report of the response.

Could such an event recur today? Cantril notes that "a pattern of circumstances providing a matrix for high suggestibility" is "by no means absent today" but that there are a number of mitigating factors: there are more channels available for cross-checking information; television dramas are less likely to be confused with reality than are radio dramas, with their appeal to the imagination; broadcasters are now aware of the potential social damage that may occur, and they screen and pretest programs with a potential for causing confusion. Nevertheless, a public television broadcast in the spring of 1975 in which a student described how an atomic bomb could be made with easily stolen materials caused a ripple of alarm in the newspapers.

In the Spring of 1979, ambiguous reports about the dangers from an accident at the Three Mile Island atomic power plant caused a spontaneous evacuation that preceded the official announcement that children and pregnant women were encouraged to leave.

If there is a significant difference between 1938 and 1980, it may be that concerns of media effects are now subtler. We are concerned about such effects as alienation caused by the media and urban isolation, the imitation of violent acts on television by children, continuing political control by those in power because of their access to large budgets, and the development of inappropriate dietary habits and, consequently, poor health because of a media-induced preference for "fun foods" of little nutritional value.

If these concerns are subtler, they are nevertheless the children of the fears our parents originally had about the effects of movies and radio. We suspect—we fear—that a major social force may be operating under the control of a few program executives, political figures, advertisers, or government officials. Even more, we suspect that a major social force may be operating without effective control from any quarter.

In this chapter we will briefly consider the major current issues concerning the effects of broadcasting on children, violence, politics, and consumerism.

Broadcasting and Children: Antisocial

It does credit to our society that there are widespread concerns about the effects of broadcasting on children. Perhaps the most widely held concern is that television is a causal factor in violence among children. So widespread was this concern that, in the spring of 1969, Senator John Pastore asked the Surgeon General to name a panel of distinguished persons to undertake to identify what harmful effects, if any, television programs have on children.

The result of the senator's request was an inquiry which lasted almost three years. The panel commissioned twenty-three research projects and many more technical papers and published what became a controversial report, which reported that the committee had found preliminary and tentative causal relations between television violence and aggressive behavior. However, the connection was too tentative to satisfy social scientists and was expressed with too many qualifications to satisfy critics of the industry.

Three years after the Surgeon General's report, Douglass Cater and Stephen Strickland published an extensive essay outlining the "evolution" and "fate" of the Surgeon General's report. It is fascinating and easy reading, and it leads the reader to a question which cannot be decided in social science terms: If some television programs cause some children to act violently some of the time, are we justified in eliminating all such content from all children's programs all of the time?

Other critics agree that there is too much violence in children's programs but point out that children also watch many programs during adult viewing hours. If televised violence is socially undesirable, these programs must also be considered. Finally, if the link between television and violence is tentative and preliminary, what evidence is needed to justify a change in social policy.

Closely linked to concerns about television and violence are those about television and delinquency. Numerous British researchers, mentioned in the bibliography, have investigated this matter and have reached conclusions as ambiguous as those reached by the Surgeon General's panel. Generally, the causes of specific behaviors appear to be too complex to reduce intelligently to a single cause. Nevertheless, television is a part of the environment of those children who are violent and/or delinquent. Some social scientists argue that all contributing factors in social change should be considered as causal. From this point of view, television is and will remain a problem for those concerned with the well-being of children.

Underlying all questions of violence and children's programming, of course, is a First Amendment question. If the FCC should, by rule or regulation, move to reduce televised violence, is there any reason it should not move to reduce "undesirable" political or religious content? The decision on how to protect children within the limits of the First Amendment is a matter for critics to ponder.

Television and Children: Pro-Social

Of course, not all of the effects of television on children are anti-social. Television introduces children to new experiences. It makes available a variety of role models. It brings them into vicarious contact with the world outside without making the linguistic or high-abstraction demands of the newspapers. There have been attempts to use television to encourage pro-social behavior, notably in the programs produced by the Children's Television Workshop.

"Sesame Street" is, of course, the best-known example of pro-social television. In it, short message units with specific instructional goals are combined with characters and puppets appealing to children to make an unusually effective program. "Sesame Street" is unusual in one other way: it was one of the first programs produced with audience research included as part of the production mechanism. Normally, in broadcasting, research is done before production to find out if there is a demand for a program and after the program is aired to find out if it is successful. The "Sesame Street" producers used research at each step of the way to find out if each unit was communicating effectively. The way in which the show was produced is admirably described in Gerald Lesser's *Children and Television: Lessons from "Sesame Street,"* a book of immense value to anyone concerned with the use of television for encouraging pro-social behavior.

The use of television or radio to support constructive behavior is not new, of course. For many years "Mr. Rogers' Neighborhood," the public television program produced in Pittsburgh, has dealt with children with a respect, sensitivity, and fairness that is often lacking in children's television—including those programs that are "pro-social." "Captain Kangaroo" is another unself-conscious attempt to deal with children seriously and without ulterior instructional motives. There are many others, of course, and the critic can provide a service for both broadcasters and children by making the issues and the role of broadcasters clear.

Children and Broadcasting: Advertising

Although most concern about television or radio and children has
been directed at the content of children's programs, some critics
and researchers have been interested in the content and effects of
advertising for children. The concern centers on problem areas:
nutrition and the development of a "sweet-tooth," which leads to
undesirable dietary habits; the use of misleading visual devices in
toy advertising to create expectations that the product will not
satisfy; the failure to give full information about products for children, such as the fact that batteries are not included or that additional dresses for a doll may be costly; advertisements that encourage children to "ask your mom" for products; the use of hosts
who may be trusted by children to deliver commercials; the over-
representation of men in both programs and commercials; and the
total amount of commercial time in children's programs.

The issue is clear and simple: critics feel that children are often
exploited by broadcasters. But the evidence to support the charge
is hard to come by—advertisements change from season to season,
and information is soon out-of-date. There are, however, some useful studies which have analyzed children's advertising. The best
single source is Action for Children's Television (46 Austin Street,
Newtonville, Massachusetts, 02160). This organization maintains
a library and can usually provide the latest information in this
changing field. As a benchmark and an indication of how the content of commercials can be analyzed, Charles Winnick's *Children's
Television Commercials* is invaluable. F. Earle Barcus's more
recent work for A.C.T. provides a current survey of children's
television.

Critics can make a useful contribution by noting abuses, by
comparing their community with data based on studies elsewhere,
and by helping to locate the elusive mean between no commercials
and consequently impoverished programs and exploitative commercials which abuse the trust of children.

Broadcasting and Politics

As we mentioned earlier, much of the concern about the effects
of broadcasting relates to its potential effect on voting behavior.
The issue was raised in a sophisticated fashion in 1968 by Richard
Nixon, whose successful campaign for the presidency included
widespread use of television and radio and use of advisers who

came from advertising backgrounds. Joe McGuiness, whose book *The Selling of the Presidency* attacked the use of sales tools in politics, argued that candidates might soon be packaged and pretested much like "Sesame Street," a new breakfast cereal, or a new automobile design.

Curiously, Richard Nixon reversed his strategy in 1972 and won reelection by emphasizing radio and using television sparingly. It was, once again, a sophisticated and effective strategy, but it did not fit the 1968 stereotype. Nevertheless, campaign consultants familiar with the commercial uses of broadcasting continue to be employed by candidates.

Although the Watergate scandal and Nixon's resignation were the major political events of the early 1970s, television played a surprisingly small part in those events. The television coverage of the Senate inquiry into the burglary and coverup, which was carried nationally during the summer of 1973, no doubt helped to create public concern about events in Washington. Aside from that coverage, however, Watergate did not relate to television, nor did television appear to influence the course of events.

The major issues concerning politics and television that are of interest to critics are:

1. Changes in the 1968 Campaign Finance Law which relate to the amounts of money which can be used for television or radio campaigns. The law appeared to be so complex in administration in the 1974 congressional campaigns that violations, some inadvertent, were frequent. The bill may be further amended before the 1976 elections. The aim of the bill is clear: to assure that all expenditures are reported and that no single candidate will have a substantial advantage in broadcast campaigning. Critics will have to observe political broadcasts and the reports of campaign financing and determine for themselves whether the law is necessary and effective.

2. Changes in Section 315 of the Communications Act of 1934 may make it possible for the major party candidates for the presidency to debate on television, as Kennedy and Nixon did in 1960. At the moment, Section 315 calls for equal time to be made available to all qualified candidates for the office. This means that all splinter party candidates have to be given time. Section 315 was suspended in 1960 and may be suspended again. If it were, many of the fears that television allows candidates to hide behind clever technicians could be

dispelled. Debates provide an unequalled opportunity to observe candidates under pressure.

3. Campaign consultants continue to be a source of controversy. Candidates obviously employ other specialists, and there is no reason to deny them the services of skilled television or radio producers. Their presence, however, does little to encourage the public to believe that the candidates are spontaneous and open in their campaigns.

The period 1968–1974 was a difficult one for those in television news concerned with politics. Some political leaders, notably then Vice President Spiro Agnew, attacked the networks as Eastern, liberal, elitist, and indifferent to the interests of "the silent majority." Others, such as Joe McGuiness, criticized Agnew and Nixon for managing the news and running slick media campaigns. Although the latter group was attacking the Nixon administration, not the media, the net effect of their criticism was to stimulate suspicion of television.

Perhaps the greatest difficulty for the critic concerned with politics and television is the abundance of predigested ideas available for repetition: News is managed by editors, we suspect. News is managed by clever politicians because newscasters are lazy. Campaign consultants can sell mediocre candidates, we have been told. The prevalence of such generalizations encourages lazy thinking about the issues. The task for critics is to remain true to their own experience and the data they can gather about events elsewhere and to minimize their dependence on generalizations.

Women and Television

There is a growing concern about the ways in which women are depicted on television. The roles they are given in television commercials, the roles they play in television dramas, and the ways in which the concerns of women are reported in television news have been the subject of concern and research. Those interested in these developments, in the absence of a single book-length summary of the literature, may find useful materials in such journals as the *Journal of Communication* and the *Journal of Broadcasting.*

The concern about the ways in which women—and other minorities—are depicted is based on the assumption that the television portrayals serve as models for many women. Others argue that television depictions create expectations: women may be expected to behave in ways consistent with what is seen on the screen.

Thus, there is a two-pronged concern about women and television: 1) a concern about what is on the screen, and 2) a concern about how what is on the screen affects its audience and/or the society generally.

The Other Effects of Broadcasting

Radio and television have been identified as causal in a variety of social situations. It has been suggested that the black revolution was stimulated by the pictures of abundance viewed daily in the homes of the poor; that regional differences are minimized by television; that radio served as a tribal drum that unified a generation in the 1960s; that radio can be used to influence musical tastes; that children learn to read earlier because of television; that television news has helped to make a better informed public than formerly existed; that television news performs a disservice by giving viewers superficial coverage of events; that television distracts viewers from satisfactions they might achieve in their real lives by occupying their time with empty fantasies; that advertising on radio and television—as well as on billboards, in magazines and newspapers, and so on—has helped create a nation of consumers.

Most of these charges seem to have sufficient validity that the response to them is usually uncritical. Yet the evidence to support the charges that such effects occur is surprisingly difficult to find. The more researchers look for proof that television causes violence, alienation, drug abuse, or consumerism, the more they find that these problems are related to many factors in today's environment, of which television is only one.

Critics have responded to this difficulty—that television and radio seem to be part of most social problems but are the primary or sole cause of none—in two different ways. Some have argued that television, particularly, should be treated as if it were causal. If the content of broadcasting is changed, they argue, other changes in the society may follow.

This was the strategy behind the attempt by the Surgeon General to popularize awareness of the link between cigarette smoking and cancer. By removing pro-smoking commercials from television and replacing them with (a lesser number of) anti-smoking spots, it was hoped that the increase in cigarette smoking could be re-versed. Unfortunately, television was apparently not sufficiently causal to bring about the desired change. Cigarette smoking has increased, both in absolute numbers and as a percentage of the population, since the advertising was removed from television.

Nevertheless, the inclination to treat television and radio as causal agents of social change persists. Perhaps this is because broadcasting, which is subject to federal regulation, is more sus-ceptible to pressure than other institutions which might also be considered "causal."

Other critics have argued that the effects of radio and television are so far-reaching that we do not have instruments capable of measuring the changes. The leading exponent of this view was Harold A. Innis, a Canadian economic historian, who argued that changes in communication—from land to sea, or from stone cutting to paper—revolutionize a society. Marshall McLuhan developed and elaborated Innis's insight in a series of publications that have baffled, frustrated, and delighted a generation of readers.

McLuhan may be frustrating to some because he views many liberal reforms as merely retrograde. Commercials, he once sug-gested, are the most interesting, the most visual, and the most innovative use to which television has been put. If that is so, why bother attempting to decrease the amount of commercials on television?

McLuhan has also noted that, from Abraham Lincoln to William Jennings Bryan, politics was dominated by people who excelled in public speaking. If our age is to be led by people who excel in the use of radio and television, why worry? Each age and culture produces leaders who excel in the media and styles dominant in the period. This ability to "see through" problems, to regard many soberly debated "issues" as merely hang-ups left over from the age of print, frustrates television critics who would like to make it respectable in a more traditional way.

McLuhan is difficult to paraphrase. His style is elliptical and he speaks in parables—he circles his conclusion rather than marching up to it in an Aristotelian progression. McLuhan also complicates matters by claiming to be neither scientist nor critic, while simul-taneously writing about science and criticism.

With that sober caveat, let us spend a moment on two of McLuhan's principal contributions to the consideration of the ef-fects of television and radio. His first contribution was to make us aware of the importance of the medium. Before McLuhan, it was common for critics to report a speech heard and a speech read in a newspaper as the same event. McLuhan pointed out that the importance of tone, audience response, pace, and inflection are minimized when a speech is reduced to print. Conversely, argument, evidence, and logical chains are emphasized when a speech is reported in print. Although earlier critics acknowledged that the medium influenced the message in the way that a rusty pipe colors the water that flows through it, McLuhan led the radical critique in arguing that the medium is at least as important—perhaps more important—than the message flowing through it. They are, he argued, inseparable.

This insight is no longer radical, though often neglected. People feel uneasy if they admit that they often watch television, not to get news or because they like specific programs but because they like to watch television. Perhaps a print illustration will make the point. I sometimes have to wait for a train when I go home after work. Standing at the platform, I often read want-ads in which I have no interest and obituaries about people who were unknown to me. Psychologists call this input-seeking behavior. I read simply because it's more pleasant than not reading. In the same way, many people watch television because it's more pleasant than not watching television. McLuhan was one of the first to observe this phenomenon.

If the medium is of crucial importance, the effects of the medium must be of considerable importance to a society. In *Understanding Media*, McLuhan elaborates his analysis of the effects of several media, including print (his *Gutenberg Galaxy* is devoted to it), the bicycle (which led to the airplane), the telegraph (which destroyed the crusading editor), the telephone, the movies, radio, and television.

McLuhan's second contribution to broadcasting was to note that art is environment consciously regarded. Laurel and Hardy movies were environment for one generation of viewers, but art for the next generation, which regarded their conventional variety show antics as sophisticated comic art. Campbell's soup cans were environment until Andy Worhol made the world conscious of their design. Coke bottles, automobiles, Ed Sullivan, and Ozzie and Harriett are all potentially art if our environment is regarded as an assortment of *objets d'art*. In this, McLuhan is merely participating in the twentieth-century revolution in literature and the arts. He was, however, the first and the only prominent critic of broadcasting to view the media as linked to the intellectual revolutions of our time. For many, the prescience and popularity of McLuhan's writing has made him something of a prophet (profit). In short, he remains unique and controversial among writers concerned with broadcasting.

More than any other critic, McLuhan has sensed the scale on which media effects may operate. While others studied the effects of the circulation of a metropolitan newspaper upon local newspapers, McLuhan was concerned with the effect of mass communication upon our sense of the importance of local politics, of community and nation. While others worried if the use of television and film production devices changed the "message" in a political broadcast, McLuhan was interested in the way in which television was changing the expectations people have of political leaders and of the ways in which they might participate in political decisions. If by "serious criticism" we mean the paying of attention to large issues rather than temporary problems, to the implications of an idea rather than its immediate application, McLuhan qualifies as one of the few serious critics of broadcasting.

McLuhan's approach may be particularly useful in dealing with the productions of those interested in experimental video: the use of studio or portable equipment for personal expression, for experimentation to discover what aesthetic achievements are possible, or for the expression of ideas or experiences which fall outside the content of conventional broadcasts, whether public or commercial. At the moment the centers of experimental video are New York and Los Angeles, but experimentation occurs wherever someone with an imaginative grasp of the possibilities of the medium has free time and access to facilities. McLuhan's willingness to let go of conventional standards, his intellectual laissez-faire-ism, are applicable to all broadcasts. He is, however, the only major critic to provide a working vocabulary and a critical stance useful in understanding productions in which such conventional criteria as "equal time," "balance," "social effects," and similar concepts are irrelevant.

The Effects of Studying Effects

Television is used and evaluated, in this country and most others, strategically. Someone usually has an interest in promoting a product, a political idea, a career, or a sport. Television is almost never innocent. It seldom exists to be merely entertaining or beautiful. Some producers and critics have argued that it should be free from commerce, but even in countries with government-sponsored systems, television and radio usually serve the interests of those who identify with the controlling ideology of the society.

Perhaps the reason television is used strategically is that it is a potentially powerful social weapon, and those who control it control power. Or perhaps it is simply because a television system is enormously expensive, and it must meet the perceived needs of large numbers of people if it is to receive their financial support. Whatever the reason, television and the radio are usually thought of strategically, in terms of their capacity for bringing about beneficial or harmful social change. The system is evaluated by its social effects, proven or suspected.

In a pluralistic society, different groups will have different interests and conflict will inevitably result. Some groups favor the growth of consumerism; others, the growth of consumption. Some will be alarmed at the potential effects of the media in causing violence; others will be indifferent to them. Since social concepts are essentially contestible, each group will attempt to define the desirability or undesirability of the effects of broadcasting in terms of its own ideology.

Given that a healthy pluralistic society handles its conflicts by understanding, critics have an important function to perform—to help their audiences understand who benefits from one analysis of media effects, and who from another. By analyzing the charges and evidence, critics can remind their audiences that the charges of media effects usually outdistance the evidence by an unhealthy margin.

Note

1. Hadley Cantril, *The Invasion from Mars* (New York: Harper and Row Torchbooks, 1966), p. vi.

Suggested Readings

Politics and Broadcasting

Chester, Edward W. *Radio, Television and American Politics.* New York: Sheed and Ward, 1969. A historical overview of broadcasting and politics from the twenties to 1968. A useful background text.

Hiebert, Ray; Robert F. Jones; John Lorenz; and Ernest A. Lotito. *Political Image Merchants: Strategies for the Seventies.* Washington, D.C.: Acropolis

Books, Ltd., 1974. A useful series of articles dealing with the 1972 campaign, ethical problems in televised politics, polling, and "image making."

Lang, Kurt, and Gladys Engle Lang. *Politics and Television*. Chicago: Quadrangle Books, 1968. A collection of papers pointing to the difference between reality and the televised image and its political consequences. Not a recent book, but the issues are basic.

McGuiness, Joe. *The Selling of the Presidency, 1968*. New York: Trident Press, 1969. A first-person narrative of his coverage of the 1968 Nixon campaign. The worst did not come to pass, but McGuiness suggests potential abuses which result from use of campaign consultants.

Mickelson, Sig. *The Electric Mirror*. New York: Dodd, Mead, and Company, 1972. One of the few scholars who feels that "television really hasn't had much effect on the national political convention." A moderate inquiry, worth reading alongside McGuiness.

Patterson, Thomas E. and Robert D. McClure. *The Unseeing Eye: The Myth of Television Power in National Politics*. New York: G.P. Putnam's Sons, 1976. A carefully argued summary of research which points to little evidence to support the popular claim that television has had large-scale effects on politics.

Rubin, Bernard. *Political Television*. Belmont, California: Wadsworth Publishing Company, 1967. A thoroughly documented narrative history of television's involvement with politics, 1960–66. A useful source book.

Broadcasting and Children: Pro-Social Messages

Lesser, Gerald S. *Children and Television*. New York: Random House, 1974. An analysis of how "Sesame Street" came about written by one of the participants. Useful for analyzing that program or for considering the design of potential future programs.

Broadcasting and Children: Advertising

Winnick, Charles; Lorne G. Williamson; Stuart F. Chuzmir; and Mariann Pezzella Winnick. *Children's Television Commercials, A Content Analysis*. New York: Praeger Publishers, 1973. A useful analysis, together with a methodology that could be used in other places. Identifies devices used in commercials and provides categories for analysis.

Barcus, F. Earle. *Television in the After-School Hours*. Newtonville, Massachusetts: Action for Children's Television, 1975. Much of the best material in this category is in report form rather than books. The reader may be best directed to Action for Children's Television where copies may be available for purchase. Among other reports available when this was prepared were studies of children's television commercials by Scott Ward and Alan Pearce.

Barcus, F. Earle. *Weekend Children's Television*. Newtonville, Massachusetts: Action for Children's Television, 1975.

Harmonay, Maureen, ed. *ACT's Guide to TV Programming for Children*, Vol. 1. Newton: Action for Children's Television. The first of a series, it focuses on "children with special needs."

Broadcasting and Children: Violence

Baker, Robert K., and Sandra J. Ball. *Mass Media and Violence*. A staff report to the National Commission on the Causes and Prevention of Violence. Volume 9. Washington, D.C.: Government Printing Office, 1969. A collection of materials that provide ammunition for both sides of the controversy.

Cater, Douglass, and Stephen Strickland. *TV Violence and the Child*. New York: Russell Sage Foundation, 1974. A useful history of the Surgeon General's report and its subsequent fate. Provides useful insights into the difficulties of relating social science to public policy.

Halloran, J. D.; R. L. Brown; and D. C. Chaney. *Television and Delinquency*. Leicester, England: Leicester University Press, 1970. Distributed in the United States by Humanities Press, New York. A balanced overview of the subject in an English setting. No similar study of the problem in an American setting is available.

Millgram, Stanley, and R. Lance Shotland. *Television and Antisocial Behavior*. New York: Academic Press, 1973. A series of experiments are reported in which attempts were made to stimulate aggressive behavior. A fascinating series of studies that have been underreported.

Noble, Grant. *Children in Front of the Small Screen*. Beverly Hills: Sage Publications, 1975. A useful summary of research through 1974.

Schramm, Wilbur; Jack Lyle; and Edwin B. Parker. *Television in the Lives of Our Children*. Palo Alto, California: Stanford University Press, 1961. A pioneering study of children and television; provides a benchmark for current discussion.

Television and Growing Up: The Impact of Televised Violence. Report to the Surgeon General of the United States Public Health Service from the Surgeon General's Scientific Advisory Committee on Television and Social Behavior. Washington, D.C.: Government Printing Office, 1971. The document that pointed to "tentative" causal relations between television and violence and became the subject of Cater and Strickland's book.

Other Effects

Bower, Robert T. *Television and the Public*. Holt, Rinehart and Winston, 1973. A survey of surveys, including ten-year comparisons in attitudes toward television. A reference book rather than a text, of considerable usefulness.

Cantril, Hadley. *The Invasion from Mars*. New York: Harper Torchbooks, 1966. The classic study of media effects. Useful in conjunction with the recording of Orson Welles' Mercury Theatre program.

Comstock, George; Steven Chaffee; Natan Katzman; Maxwell McCombs and Donald Roberts, eds. *Television and Human Behavior*. New York: Columbia University Press, 1978. The most recent and best one-volume summary of research on the effects of television.

Crosby, Harry H., and George R. Bond. *The McLuhan Explosion*. New York: American Book Company, 1968. A collection of reviews of McLuhan's books that leave the reader amused and bewildered.

McLuhan, Marshall. *The Gutenberg Galaxy*. Toronto: University of Toronto Press, 1962. The best analysis of how print influenced the consciousness, language, and development of Western Europe.

McLuhan, Marshall. *The Mechanical Bride*. Boston: Beacon Press, 1951. A campy tour of pop culture by a guide who is aware of its mythic function for audiences.

McLuhan, Marshall. *Through the Vanishing Point*. With Harley Parker. New York: Harper and Row, 1968. A series of probes and puns, including a valuable essay, "The Emperor's New Clothes." In this study, he points out the path taken by painters who have moved from a single point of view to a more inclusive aesthetic.

McLuhan, Marshall. *Understanding Media*. New York: McGraw-Hill, 1964. His most intelligible and unsurpassed study of television, radio, film, etc.

Schwartz, Tony. *The Responsive Chord*. Garden City, New York: Anchor Books, 1974. An analysis of how radio and television influence us, by a producer with a McLuhan consciousness.

Sterling, Christopher and Timothy R. Haight. *The Mass Media: Aspen Institute Guide to Communication Industry Trends*. New York: Praeger, 1978. The most concise single source of information about the media size, corporate relationships, audience sizes, etc.

Wells, Alan, ed. *Mass Media and Society*. Palo Alto: Mayfield Publishing Company, 1975. A collection of essays concerning the social and political effects of the mass media. Useful if read in conjunction with Comstock.

Beyond the Wasteland

On May 9, 1961, Newton N. Minow, then Chairman of the Federal Communications Commission, spoke before the National Association of Broadcasters. He invited the broadcasters to view their television stations from sign-on to sign-off. "I assure you," he said, "that you will observe a vast wasteland."

The phrase was quickly reported by the press and became a catch-word in popular discussions of television. The echo of the despair expressed in Eliot's poem attracted intellectuals who found it an apt summary of their disdain of the new medium.

Minow went on to identify the causes of the wasteland: the pursuit of ratings, the need to hold mass audiences, the high cost of programs, the need for programs, the demands of advertisers. His analysis was less widely reported, however, than the catchy title of his speech and his threatening words that "there is nothing permanent or sacred about a broadcast license."

That speech may serve as a freeze-frame of the period: one of President Kennedy's brightest appointees speaking out against things as they were and in favor of balance, the serving of many interests, quality programs, and public broadcasting.

Nearly fifteen years have passed since that speech, and it seems curiously elitist in its concern with quality, and surprisingly current in identifying the issues that are still unresolved: concentration of control, the cost of programs, the concern with ratings, and the tyranny of majority taste and the networks. Other bright and liberal commissioners have served on the FCC and, in some cases, led it, but the problems remain.

Why, one may ask, have some issues remained constant over such a comparatively long period of time? One reason is that the underlying problems, such as the high cost of television program production, have remained obstacles to those who would change the system. As long as production costs are high, television programs will have to be seen by large numbers of people—either at one time or as a sum of many reruns—in order to keep the cost-per-viewer reasonably low. This leads inevitably to a concern with maximizing audience size.

Some problems remain because of false analyses of their causes. Advertisers were often accused of using their influence to assure that bland programs which presented noncontroversial settings for commercials dominated the schedules of networks and stations. As advertisers withdrew from program-length sponsorship and merely bought short spot announcements in programs, however, the quality of the programs did not change to any great degree.

If the sponsors were not to blame, some argued, it must be the "three men in New York"—one at each network—who are responsible for network program decisions. But, when prime evening time was returned to local stations because of the Prime Time Access Rule, programming did not improve in most markets. Game shows were offered by local broadcasters more often than any other kind of program. Concentration of control, though perhaps undesirable for other reasons, did not appear to be the cause of mediocrity.

And so television remains a conundrum, a puzzle, and a frustration to the critic. Why do so many people remain loyal audience members of a medium which sets so low a standard of excellence?

The problem is not uniquely American. In the United Kingdom, despite a nearly forty-year monopoly by the British Broadcasting Corporation, which set about self-consciously to raise public taste, audience interest in popular music and light television programming resulted in the introduction of alternative services in both radio and television. England presents a particularly interesting puzzle for those interested in public taste, because the Labor Party, which draws its support from those who are in the majority in commercial program audiences, has opposed the growth of the commercial system for economic reasons.

It may be that the cultivation of excellence in broadcasting can only be achieved if programs and delivery systems are financed independently of audience preferences, but, in an age characterized by increasing populism, such solutions are not likely to be well received.

What Happened to Excellence?

Although we have emphasized the constancy of some problems, such as the concern with audience size or program cost, there have been important changes in the ways in which criticism of broadcasting is phrased. Perhaps the most important is the change from a concern with *quality*, which was widespread in the 1950s and 1960s, to a concern with *effects*.

The concern with effects has had two results. As was mentioned earlier, critics have often talked about the negative effects: imitative violence, stereotyping of minorities, and the manipulation of children by advertisers. The result of this interest in effects has been censorious. Pressure groups attempt to eliminate the programs which produce, or may produce, the undesired effect.

Others, also concerned with effects, have emphasized the possibilities inherent in radio and television for bringing about pro-social effects. The result has been such programs as "Sesame Street," which has been widely praised for bringing about accelerated learning of letters. "Zoom" has been praised for presenting desirable models of personal relations which may be imitated by viewers. "Feeling Good" was an attempt to improve the health and nutrition of audience members by presenting information and models for imitation.

Although public television producers are more concerned with pro-social effects because their funding agencies are interested in such possibilities, commercial broadcasters have also been interested in determining if their programs have pro-social effects. "Fat Albert," for instance, was the object of an investigation to determine what kinds of "messages" were perceived by members of the audience.

The concern with effects is interesting because of the regulatory problems it raises. It is the 1970s corollary of the problem raised by the "wasteland" speech: Who, we argued then, was to determine what was qualitatively desirable? For the seventies the problem is, Who should determine what kinds of effects should be encouraged or discouraged—the audience, by voting with its on-off switch; regulatory agencies, responding to a variety of pressure groups; or broadcasters, responding to audiences, funding groups (whether commercial or foundation or governmental), and their long-range concern with keeping their licenses?

The Natural Relation

Philosopher Stanley Cavell, explaining why he wrote a book about film, wrote that for twenty-five years going to films was a normal part of his week. It would, he said, "no more have occurred to me to write a study of movies than to write my autobiography."[1]

Having written the book, he wondered, "What broke my natural relation to movies?" The estrangement from a medium which finds its expression in the need to philosophize about it is a com-com experience in the popular arts. The dominance of the newspaper in the nineteenth century was followed by an interest in the organization, functions, and effects of the press that has resulted in a rigorous academic field of study. Similarly, the discovery that the movies attended uncritically by a generation were interesting to analyze resulted in the explosion of film books, magazines, and criticism in the 1960s. Something, as Cavell observed, happened to break the natural relation.

Marshall McLuhan has noted the breakdown of the "natural relation" and described it in different terms. He argues that those things about which we are not self-conscious—movies in the thirties, coke bottles in the forties—are "environment." When we become self-conscious of our reactions to them, they become "art." One function of the artist is to shatter the natural relation, to make us aware of the quality of everyday products (Andy Worhol or Claes Oldenberg), sounds (John Cage), or clothes (the unsung genius who noticed that blue jeans have visual and tactile qualities and take on something of the experience of the wearer). Blue jeans, urban sounds, motorcycle engines, and Coca Cola bottles were once environment. The natural relation was broken, however, and these things are now considered art.

Most people retain their natural relation to television. Although viewers give token support to charges of mediocrity, they continue to view repetitive programs. Although they are concerned about effects, they continue to view programs containing representations of reality that are violent and that emphasize dominance and conflict. Radio and television may be arts to the minority that is self-conscious—"Star Trek" freaks and old radio show buffs—but for most people it was never a wasteland and they are not yet arts. It is the role of critics to break the natural relation, to raise the self-consciousness of viewers and listeners.

The Problems of Plenitude

Although the issues in broadcast criticism have been relatively constant, aside from the change from a concern with quality to a concern with effects, there has been a quiet revolution in the industry. Where once the American public was served by less than a thousand AM radio stations, there are now more than five thousand AM, FM, UHF-television and VHF-television stations. The number of channels of information available to us has increased more than fivefold and has added the dimensions of sight, color, and stereo sound.

This radical increase in service has attracted little attention because the largest prime-time audience has remained faithful to network television. However, AM radio audiences have recovered from the low levels of the 1950s (after the introduction of television), and FM radio is rapidly increasing the size of the audience it serves. Cable television offers a future in which the number of channels may be further increased.

In the recent past the FCC has followed policies aimed at preventing a breakdown of the dominant commercial broadcast services. A breakthrough, rather than a breakdown, in communication services may be approaching. The ways in which this plenitude is used will be a major issue for critics in the near future. Of immediate concern is the role of the FCC. Should it protect the established services or encourage cable, satellite, laser, or other distribution systems?

Beyond the Wasteland

We began by suggesting that Newton Minow's comments on the "wasteland" could serve as a tableaux of the 1960s. It was the age of big cars, big networks, big advertising budgets, and big regulatory agencies. Liberal reformers, from Newton Minow to Nicholas Johnson, made little perceptible change in the policies or contents of American broadcasting.

What lies ahead? Will the same issues be raised by future reformers, or will there be a radically different system with different problems? Honesty and modesty make it necessary to attach a disclaimer to any discussion of the future—it simply is impossible to know. Yet there are some trends which deserve the attention of critics:

1. The creation of a new government agency, the National Telecommunications and Information Agency (NTIA) provides a center for the planning of communication policy that does not have a vested interest in protecting the existing system.
2. The development of new channels may lead to opportunities for new voices to be heard or, if badly administered, a repetition of the same voices heard now in the existing channels.
3. The potential profit from any widely accepted innovation—interactive cable, direct satellite-to-home transmission—is enormous.

4. As each change has occurred in broadcasting technology
   FM, color, video tape recording—the existing institutions
   have been incorporated in the new service. This may not
   occur in the future. The networks, for instance, may not be
   needed for the transmission of entertainment programs;
   newspapers may not be needed if videotext can be improved.

All of the observations listed above are modest and conservative
in the sense that they assume the continuity of society in approxi-
mately the form that we know it. There are other factors which
may move the social ground upon which the communication
system is built.

For instance, there is a widespread renewal of interest in religion and its relation to everyday life. This interest often occurs
outside established religions and takes the form of studies in Yoga,
participation in the Human Potential Movement, or the reading of
sacred texts from other cultures. This interest has had little effect
on our public life because it exists largely in small organizations:
a group of friends, a class, or a popular book by an anthropologist
about his exploration of the uses of peyote by Indians. Such interests and activities may seem socially negligible, but they are
widespread.

Many splinter groups, with a substantial audience among the
young, are challenging the separation of the religions from other
institutions in public life. Secularization has been one of the concepts which freed scientific, corporate, and university life from
the shackles of the past. Theodore Roszak has argued,

> Now all this is changing. There is a strange, new radicalism abroad
> which refuses to respect the conventions of secular thought and
> value, which insists on making the visionary powers a central
> point of political reference.[2]

This thrust toward integrating vision and everyday life is new.
It is easy to dismiss. But let us imagine some possible consequences
if large numbers of people followed the path toward a society im-
bued with religious values. One might expect the concept of objectivity in institutional planning to be sacrificed for the immediate needs of those concerned with it. The "new journalism" of
the 1960s challenged the concept of objectivity, and advocacy—
formally acknowledged rather than implied advocacy—is now
more common. What if broadcast journalists, in large numbers,
abandoned objectivity as a goal and made an effort to report the
"truth" of their own experiences of events? Can we imagine the

production of an advertisement as a religious exercise in which the aim is to bring about as total as possible a disclosure between the maker of a product and the consumer?

One slips into parody attempting to describe future models for communication systems. But "new historians" are arguing for the validity of the subjective experience of history, and "new economists" are arguing that economic values cannot—perhaps should not—be objectified at the expense of the subjective experience of the people concerned. Perhaps we are experiencing a humanizing of nineteenth-century social, economic, and religious views in which vision and reality were separated. Perhaps we are experiencing the early tremors of a larger seismic disturbance.

We are now at the far side of the wasteland. The Great Society and the war which blossomed with it are behind us. What lies beyond the wasteland is unknown. Whatever communication systems develop must fit the society of that future time. It is the job of critics to note where they fit and where they pinch.

Notes

1. Stanley Cavell, *The World Viewed* (New York: Viking Press, 1971), p. ix.

2. Theodore Roszak, *Where the Wasteland Ends* (Garden City, New York: Doubleday & Company, 1972), pp. xxi-xxii.

Afterword

The criticism of radio and television in the United States developed at the same time as public awareness of the vast budgets, audiences, and possible effects of broadcasting. As a consequence, American critics, with occasional notable exceptions, have been less interested in the quality of the programming and its cultural role than in the issues and celebrities which have provided readers for their work.

It does not have to be this way. Gilbert Seldes has suggested ways in which specific programs may be considered as illustrations of larger issues. But the widespread concern with the current, the topical, may in itself prove fatal to criticism. By emphasizing a series of seemingly discrete issues as they appear, the critic may miss the assumptions underlying them all.

Raymond Williams, the English critic, has written that most criticism falls into two categories. The first is *technological determinism*, which assumes that technological innovations are causes of social change (the automobile caused the growth of suburbs; the printing press caused modern, bureaucratic, literate society; the transistor caused the development of youth culture; etc.).[1] The second, *symptomatic technology*, "appears" less deterministic because it assumes that technological changes are the symptoms of large-scale changes determined by other forces. Criticism of American broadcasting can be neatly pigeon-holed into Williams's two categories: those who argue that television is the cause of social change (rising crime, divorce rates, etc.) and those who see radio and television as symptoms of a society characterized by increasing alienation, passivity, and rootlessness.

Williams suggests that it is possible to establish a third critical position. Communication technologies, he argues, were intentionally developed in response to problems perceived in many different countries.

> The decisive and earlier transformation of industrial production, and its new social forms, which had grown out of a long history

110

of capital accumulation and working technical improvement, created new needs but also new possibilities, and the communications systems, down to television, were their intrinsic outcome.[2]

One need not accept Williams's conclusions to appreciate his major contribution: he has stepped back from "the issues" and transcended the smaller questions by framing them in a larger one. Rather than asking, "Does television cause violence?" or "Is violence on television a symptom of violence elsewhere in the society?" he asserts, "If we are to begin to approach any real study of effects, we shall have to return to a scientific consideration of causes."[3]

This kind of meta-criticism (the criticism of criticism) is lacking on the American scene. We badly need critics who are able not only to deal with the issues raised earlier in this paper but to frame those issues in larger cultural criticism.

If meta-critics are concerned with framing and evaluating the issues of the day in a larger context, there is another kind of criticism which relates radio and television to issues which transcend the media and the day, perhaps even the age. Let us, for convenience, call it "transcendent criticism." Such critics might begin with a general concern and relate it to the media. For instance, sociologist Robert Nisbet has written,

> Pluralist society is free society exactly in proportion to its ability to protect as large a domain as possible that is governed by the informal, spontaneous, custom-derived, and tradition-sanctioned habits of the mind rather than by the dictates, however rationalized, of government and judiciary. Law is vital—formal, statute law—but when every relationship in society becomes a potentially legal relationship, expressed in adversary fashion, the very juices of the social bond dry up, the social impulse atrophies.[4]

In 1980 we are experiencing a fundamentalist revival: patriotism, military strength and a reduced lifestyle reflecting reduced consumption of oil are the coins of social interaction. Yet, the technological breakthroughs which give greater choice to consumers and which make national control of communications more difficult are also with us. It seems unlikely that we can turn back in our political life while our communication systems develop. Such meta-problems call for the active involvement of the critic in our everyday life.

This book has been organized around the critical issues of the day in broadcasting. These are, after all, the matters which hold our attention from day to day. If the reader not only deals with the issues but questions whether they are issues (meta-criticism) or relates them to larger and more durable concerns (transcendent criticism), the result will be both better understanding of television and insight into the culture in which we participate.

Notes

1. Raymond Williams, *Technology and Cultural Form* (New York: Schocken Books, 1975), p. 13.

2. Ibid., p. 19.

3. Ibid., p. 122.

4. Robert Nisbet, *The Twilight of Authority* (New York: Oxford University Press, 1975), p. 240.

DATE DUE